Older Volunteers in Church and Community

Older Volunteers in Church and Community

A Manual for Ministry

Paul B. Maves

Illustrated by Helen Hamilton

Judson Press ® Valley Forge

Older Volunteers in Church and Community

Copyright © 1981
Judson Press, Valley Forge, PA 19481

Unless otherwise indicated, Bible quotations in this volume are from the Revised
Standard Version of the Bible, copyrighted 1946, 1952, 1971, 1973 © by the
Division of Christian Education of the National Council of the Churches of Christ
in the United States of America, and are used by permission.

Library of Congress Cataloging in Publication Data

Maves, Paul B.
    Older volunteers in church and community.

    Bibliography: p.
    1. Aged volunteers in social service—United States.   2. Aged—Services for—
United States.   3. Church work with the aged.   4. Aged—Religious
life.   I. Title.
HV1465.M38   361.7′5   80-28093
ISBN 0-8170-0889-6

The name JUDSON PRESS is registered as a trademark in the U. S. Patent
Office. Printed in the U. S. A. ✳

Contents

Foreword   **7**

SECTION I   Perspectives on the Ministry of Older Volunteers

Chapters

1 Older People as Volunteers   **11**
2 The Church as a Volunteer Ministry   **17**
3 The Professional and the Volunteer   **23**
4 Motivating Volunteers to Serve   **29**

SECTION II   Managing Volunteer Ministries with Older People

Chapters

5 Set the Stage for Ministry   **39**
6 Call Volunteers into Ministry   **55**
7 Equip Volunteers for Ministry   **63**
8 A Kit of Leadership Training Sessions   **69**
9 Supervision—To Build Up the Body of Christ for Mission   **77**

Bibliography   **87**
Appendix A   Organizations Concerned with Volunteers   **89**
Appendix B   Guidelines for Proposal Writing   **91**

Foreword

If you are committed to the ministry of older people and are perplexed about how to help that ministry happen, this manual is addressed to you. It suggests ways in which you and those who have retired can experience meaningful living in Christian service.

If you are aware of needs for community services that cry out to be met and you wonder who might answer, or if the church itself needs volunteers, this manual is for you. It points to a vast potential for ministry by older adults.

Are you a pastor of a local church, head of a church school or of an organization, director of a church-sponsored community service agency, coordinator of volunteers somewhere? This manual is for you.

While this manual relates to volunteers of all ages, it is focused specifically on *older* volunteers, particularly those who have retired.

This manual is unique in yet another way. It was requested by a conference of 250 older members of American Baptist churches and has been produced by older adults. I, the author, am a retired seminary professor, now reemployed. The consultant to this project is a retired public school principal, Ernest Downs, who had many volunteers working in his school.

The director of the Alternatives for the Aging program of American Baptist Churches' Board of National Ministries, who, along with a writers' conference group, lent a hand in publishing this manual, also is a retiree from seminary teaching. A major contributor to the planning of the manual is a retired administrator of American Baptist Churches' Department of Ministry with Children, currently a volunteer in church and community enterprises.

As for me, a lifetime of involvement as a volunteer in a variety of church and community programs—as well as more than thirty-five years of observation, research, and personal experience in working with older people—underlie this manual. My present appointments as special consultant on aging to the Division of Health and Welfare of the Board of Global Ministries of the United Methodist Church and as director of the National Shepherds Center Development Project have enabled me to observe the functioning of programs in a variety of settings which depend upon the involvement of older people as volunteers. My observations constitute much of the background for this book.

You, the reader, have two choices in using this book. You may read it through from the beginning as a regular text about older volunteers. Or you may prefer to turn immediately to the second section on managing volunteer ministries to read those parts of primary interest to you. The pages of the book have been punched so that you may put them in a loose-leaf binder and intermingle the pages with your notes, clippings, and additional material to serve you as a workbook. You may want to mark the sections of the book with tabs so that you can turn quickly to a specific topic.

As I reflect on my own experiences of involvement as a volunteer or as a professional working with volunteers, and as I observe churches and church-sponsored social agencies in action, I am aware of how intuitively, spontaneously, and informally all such institutions usually operate.

In light of all of that, this manual may seem coldly formal and ponderous, unwieldy and not quite focused on the situation of a particular congregation or agency.

As an older adult who has experienced the profound gratification of continued social involvement, I believe that we must become much more conscious, intentional, and skillful in building communities that enable more older persons to fulfill their ministry. I hope that this manual will serve as a guide toward that objective. The suggestions made here will need to be adapted, fleshed out, and have life breathed into them until they are right for your situation.

Although this manual was requested by American Baptist laity and its development was financed by the Board of National Ministries of the American Baptist Churches, it is offered to all persons who appreciate their retirement years as ''a time of grace'' and seek to share without pay the gifts and resources given them.

Perspectives on the Ministry of Older Volunteers

Before we plunge into the nitty-gritty questions of finding, recruiting, motivating, training, commissioning, supervising, and rewarding volunteers, we need to be clear about the role of older people as volunteers, the nature of the church as a ministering community, the relations between the professional and the volunteer, and the motivations which impel persons to volunteer or which deter them from getting involved.

Chapter 1

Older People as Volunteers

Every Thursday morning, as he has done for the last six years, Mr. D. gets into his car, drives to his church, picks up ten thermoplastic trays, and delivers hot lunches to ten homebound persons. Such faithfulness is remarkable. But what is even more remarkable is that Mr. D. is eighty-eight years old. Delivering meals-on-wheels is just one of the services Mr. D. renders in the community through his church.

Mrs. I., who is eighty-four, spends twelve hours every Tuesday as a volunteer at the city hospital, which she has been doing for eight years. She retired at age sixty-seven from a thirty-five-year career as a nurse's aide. After retirement she worked as an in-home nurse's aide for three years. During that time she has reared six children, and cared periodically for eighteen grandchildren, twenty-three great-grandchildren, and seven great-great-grandchildren. She is active in a "prayer band," the church choir, the missionary group, and the women's Bible class of the church to which she has belonged for forty-four years. She plans to work at the hospital as long as she is able. She gets her drive and focus for her work through the church fellowship and worship.

Four women, long housebound by physical handicaps, are a prayer support group for the people of a nearby church who keep them up to date by delivering to them a weekly prayer list and report on the enterprises of the congregation. As an intercessory prayer group, these housebound volunteers are an integral part of the church's mission.

Eight retired citizens (from sixty-five to eighty) have become trained leaders of personal growth groups for older adults which meet weekly at a continuing education center, sponsored by a midwest university.

"Not only remarkable but also quite unusual," you say. Not so unusual as you might think. These stories could be duplicated many times over.

We know of a city council that has an advisory board of senior citizens ranging in age from 82 to 101. Increasingly, older people are performing significant volunteer service in every kind of setting, from their local church to overseas missions, from the Retired Senior Volunteer Programs in the local community to the Peace Corps. Older people now constitute a major growing pool of human resources available today for volunteer service, a great untapped reservoir of human talent which society can ill afford to ignore. Beyond that, we who are older know that older people need to have a meaningful and significant role in family and society. We need to be needed and wanted. We need to be useful. We need to experience ourselves as contributors, making a difference to somebody in some sort of way. Older people, just as all others, are called by God to love and to praise through work and worship, wherever we may be, whatever our condition. As Christians we know our value because of God's love for us and our reciprocal loving.

Our zest for living is enhanced as we engage meaningfully in the events of the day and experience ourselves as still a part of the whole of God's creation.

More than twenty-three million persons over age sixty-five live in the United States. We older people constitute 11 percent of the whole. We number more than 15 percent of the eligible voters. The shift in the age structure of our society is dramatically represented in the following figure:

The Demographic Shift in the U.S., 1910–2025[1]

in 1910	by 1985	by 2025
14% were youth 18–24		17% will be 65 plus
	12% both youth and elderly	
4% were age 65 and over		9% will be youth

[1]Percentages are derived from information in U.S. Bureau of the Census, *Current Population Reports,* Series P-25, No. 311, ''Estimates of the Population of the United States, by Single Years of Age, Color, and Sex: 1900 to 1959'' (Washington, D.C.: U.S. Government Printing Office, 1965), pp. 102-103; and Series P-25, No. 704, ''Projections of the Population of the United States: 1977 to 2050'' (Washington, D.C.: U.S. Government Printing Office, 1977), p. 4.

But note—even though by age we are 11 percent of the population, we are only 7 percent of America's volunteers. Since we may allocate time as we wish and have more free time than younger people, why are we not more numerous?

After retirement at sixty-five, an increasing number of persons will have fifteen to thirty years to live. Furthermore, today's older people are generally healthier, better educated, and more active than those of previous generations. Most of us are not helpless, senile dodderers, good for nothing but rocking lives away beside the stove or on the front porch. Studies show that 80 to 85 percent of us are functionally healthy and able to do whatever we need to do. We are independent and active, all the more so by the use of eyeglasses, hearing aids, and canes. When we have transportation, public or private, we can be active in the community in many different ways.

Consider also the range of talent and skill possessed by us. We are the survivors! We have learned to cope. Some of us have had extensive formal education. Many have developed valued skills through thirty to forty years of on-the-job training. We have run households and reared children. Some have traveled extensively. Some have been avid readers for sixty or more years. We have lived through many different kinds of experiences and have met many different kinds of people. So perspectives and backgrounds vary widely. Among us are represented all of the cultures of the world. We are the most heterogeneous, most accomplished group, most life-enriched segment of the population. We've experienced more decades, lived through more changes, know more traditions, and have a longer history than anybody else alive. Since we have a longer history, we have a shorter future. That makes time all the more precious—to be used well, enjoyed, and not trivialized.

Is it fortuitous or dare we think it part of God's design that the number of capable older people with unscheduled time is increasing just when a growing number of women (who have been this country's main block of volunteers) are entering the job market from choice or for economic reasons and no longer are available for voluntary service?

Older People in Volunteer Services

Who is this growing number of older people who are significantly involved in volunteer activities? Many are working in federally aided programs. For example, in January of 1977 there were over 14,000 Foster Grandparents serving in 182 projects in all the states, Puerto Rico, and the Virgin Islands, giving four hours a day five days a week to each of two children, doing such things as feeding and dressing them, playing games, reading, telling stories, taking them on expeditions, and helping with physical and speech therapy. There were nearly 230,000 volunteers in the Retired Senior Volunteer Programs (RSVP) in 680 projects working in courts, schools, libraries, day care centers, hospitals, nursing homes, and other community agencies. Volunteers in Service to America (VISTA) included about 500 persons 55 years of age and older working in impoverished urban and rural areas on a subsistence allowance basis. In 1975, 467 persons 51 years and older were in the Peace Corps, including 63 persons between the ages of 71 and 80, serving overseas for a small stipend. At the end of 1976, over 1,900 volunteers were serving in 48 projects in the Senior Companion Program. In January, 1977, approximately 6,850 retired businessmen and businesswomen were in the Service Corps of Retired Executives as consultants to owners and managers of small businesses.[2]

Older People Have a Vocation

Nonetheless, many older people get the message that they are of no use any more, that no one

[2]*HEW Fact Sheet*, No. (OHDS) 77-2-233 (Washington, D.C.: U.S. Department of Health, Education, and Welfare, Office of Human Development, Administration on Aging).

needs them, that there is nothing anyone wants them to do which they feel they can do. For many, retirement is likened to being laid on a shelf or put out to pasture. Many older people, after their retirement, say they want something *meaningful* to do, some way to spend their time that has value for others.

The question "What on earth am I good for?" is answered by the Christian doctrine of vocation: Every person born is created in God's image and meant to participate in God's ongoing creative work. For each person there is a destiny; for each one God has the intention that in ways appropriate for him or her each will learn to love as God loves even though this takes a lifetime of learning. A function of the church is to help people so to love—even unto death. No dropouts at sixty-five!

The charter for this calling is to be found in two documents. One is the great commandment which calls us to love the Lord our God with all our beings and to love our neighbor as ourselves. (See Matthew 22:37-39.) The other is the Great Commission which sends us out to "make disciples of all nations . . . teaching them to observe all that [the Lord has] commanded" (Matthew 28:19-20).

This calling is to all persons. It is for life. There is no retirement from God's calling. As long as we live, we are to manifest love to God and to others, wherever we may be, whatever condition we may be in. We are most fulfilled when we respond affirmatively to this calling. To see this as a commandment is to recognize that this is what reality requires for us to become most fully human, to be the persons God created us to be.

Jitsuo Morikawa says:

Ministry of the laity is the total human enterprise, in collaboration with God, in the reshaping of human history toward the New Creation. Ministry is the fundamental nature and purpose to which God has called the whole human family. Laity means the whole people of God, for in God's perspective, God has the whole of humankind in view as God's people. Therefore, when Hendrik Kraemer calls for a Copernican revolution in our understanding of ministry, it really means explosion of the miniscule conception of the ministry of the clergy, to the larger horizon of the whole worshipping community and finally to the farthest reaches of the whole human family.[3]

The uncommitted life of the person who keeps all options open and avoids entangling relationships is an empty and sterile life. Talent that is invested increases. Talent that is hoarded shrinks. "Use it or lose it" is a law of life.

Given the fact that human beings are created for relationships that build community, given the further fact that we spend five and six decades learning how to do that, is it any wonder that the human psyche sickens when the door to community is suddenly closed or threatens to close due to retirement, poverty, ill health, death of spouse, loss of family, or deprivation of transportation that is an essential for togetherness when neighborhood living is destroyed?

Older Volunteers Are Different

When working with older volunteers, we need to keep in mind several characteristics which differentiate us from younger volunteers.

The first and most obvious, of course, is that we may have larger blocks of discretionary time which we seek to fill with meaningful and satisfying activity.

The second is that usually we will respond to opportunities which use the skills we have mastered in our occupations and which will call on us to do what we have been doing.[4] Our volunteering, at least initially, is more likely to be for something that is a continuation of some aspect of our experience—something we already know and value in ourselves. This is just the opposite

of younger volunteers who frequently look to their volunteer activities for new dimensions of experience. A retired clinical psychologist reported with some frustration, "My church has never asked me to do in the church what I am best equipped to do." This is not to be construed to mean that older people don't welcome new opportunities.

The third is that we have had lots of experience and training on which to draw. This has furnished us with a large repertoire of options for coping with problems and solving them. Generally this means that we have gained considerable practical judgment and are not so likely to act impulsively or rashly.

Fourth, allowance must be made in many cases for flexibility in schedules. Many do want a certain amount of freedom to travel or to visit kinfolk; so we welcome teaming up with other volunteers or signing up for limited contracts with a clear understanding about the commitment.

Fifth, it has been demonstrated that once we accept an assignment, we are likely to be more responsible and dependable than younger workers. It's on the record that we exhibit less absenteeism in the main than younger workers. The experience of Bankers Life and Casualty Company,[5] which has no mandatory retirement age and hires older persons, supports this.

Finally, some allowances must be made for any changes in our physical capacities. Some of us drive cars during the day but do not like to drive at night because some older eyes do not adjust as rapidly to changes from light to dark and do not perceive objects distinctly in dim light. Some older persons no longer drive at all and therefore must depend upon public transportation. Older volunteer handymen should not be expected to climb ladders and work on roofs. Those of us who are hard of hearing can do many things which

[3]Jitsuo Morikawa, "Ministry of the Whole People of God" in *Ministry of the Laity Packet* (Valley Forge: American Baptist National Ministries, 1979).

[4]See Barbara P. Payne, "The Older Volunteer: Social Role Continuity and Development," *The Gerontologist,* vol. 17, no. 4 (August, 1977), pp. 355-361.

[5]See *Bankers' Experience with Over-65 Workers,* available from Bankers Life and Casualty Company, 4444 W. Lawrence Avenue, Chicago, IL 60630.

do not involve a great deal of conversation and the accurate oral reception of information. In other words, take note of who we are, but don't assume that decreased sensory capacity incapacitates us for everything!

Barriers to Involving Older Volunteers

In the light of all these factors, why have older people been overlooked so often in the recruitment of volunteers? Why are so many of us sitting on the sidelines? Why are we so often thought of as objects to be ministered to and taken care of rather than as persons in ministry?

Perhaps, for one thing, many persons in society are not aware of how the older population has changed. In the past, older people were fewer in number, did not live as long, and health tended to break down much earlier.

But probably more than anything else, the bypassing of older adults is due to the many negative myths about aging uncritically held as truths, myths which have little relation to reality, but which act as distorting screens.

Dr. Robert Butler, the distinguished psychiatrist who is director of the National Institute on Aging in the National Institute of Health at Bethesda, Maryland, lists a number of erroneous images of aging that act as barriers to prevent the community from giving older people a significant place in society. These deter also the elderly themselves from the full expression of their power to live fully. Some of the most damaging myths (untruths and prejudices) Butler lists are the following.[6]

Myth No. 1: Aging is measurable by the number of years one lives.

Fact: Different persons age at different rates. Different organs in the body age at different rates. It cannot be assumed that just because a

[6]Robert Butler, "Successful Aging," *Mental Health*, Summer, 1974. See also his book *Why Survive? Being Old in America* (New York: Harper & Row, Publishers, Inc., 1975), pp. 7-12.

person has lived a certain number of years, his or her capacities have diminished a particular amount.

Myth No. 2: Older people are unproductive.

Fact: Studies have shown that older workers tend to be more dependable than younger workers, miss fewer days of work, and in most occupations can perform as well as those of other ages.

Myth No. 3: Older people want to disengage from life and activity.

Fact: Some do, because they have had bad experiences with work and relationships and because they have been led to believe that disengagement is what is expected of them. Most do not. They are looking for interesting and rewarding ways to spend their time. They are eager to maintain relationships, make new friends, and learn new skills.

Myth No. 4: Older people are set in their ways and will not change.

Fact: Rigidness and conservatism vs. flexibility and liberalism are functions of personality structure and social environment rather than of age.

Myth No. 5: Older people inevitably become senile and decline into a second childhood.

Fact: Many of the patterns of behavior lumped under the heading of senility may be caused by anxiety and depression over losses and strains of adjustment. Others may be caused by the overuse of drugs or alcoholism in coping with depression. Malnutrition and physical illness also can lead to a cutting off of the blood supply to the brain and so produce behavior such as forgetfulness and confusion. Organic brain damage is experienced by only 5 to 10 percent of older people. New research shows promise of preventing many of the diseases which cause the so-called problems of old age.

Myth No. 6: Older people are serene, carefree, and placid.

Fact: Older people tend to undergo more

stress than those of any other group. These stresses are associated with enforced and unwanted retirement, the loss of spouse through death or divorce, the death of friends, the losses associated with diseases which reduce capacity to function and the fear of socially imposed poverty after a lifetime of continuous serving. Older people commit 25 percent of the suicides in the United States. It has been estimated that as many as two-thirds of all older people at some time or other experience reactive depression due to losses and threatened losses. Psychosomatic illnesses, paranoia, irritability, and garrulousness are some of the responses to these stresses.

Dr. Butler has coined the term "ageism" to refer to these negative images which cause society to discriminate against older people. Such discrimination takes the form of mandatory retirement at a fixed age, dropping older people from leadership, ignoring them in significant decision making and in planning programs, and often treating them in the mass media as buffoons.

Some of the discrimination against and avoidance of older persons stems from younger persons' unresolved conflicts with older authority figures (parents especially) and from their own fear of aging. Because of these negative views and expectations of the old, many people live in fear of their own aging and tend to avoid anything and anyone who would remind them of their own future. It's just easier to forget about the old! Thus, "old" for some people is a synonym for "drop out."

In Summary

We need to look at older persons without the blinders of unexamined and erroneous assumptions. We need to become aware of the vast array of talent possessed by the elderly. We need to recall that every person is called to lifelong ministry. Therefore, we need to consider the many ways older persons may participate with those of other ages in ministry as volunteers.

Chapter 2

The Church as a Volunteer Ministry

The involvement of volunteers in ministry is of the very essence of the church's nature. The church is not a clinic where a handful of professionals take care of vast numbers of sick and needy patients. It is a ministering community wherein all of the members who have experienced the love manifested in Jesus Christ respond by loving others in his name. Church members not only covenant to care for one another but also are committed to a concern for all of humankind.

Called to Be a Ministering Community

Jesus, speaking of the multitudes, said, "I came that they may have life, and have it abundantly" (John 10:10). He also said, quoting the prophet Isaiah,

The Spirit of the Lord is upon me,
because he has anointed me to preach good news to
    the poor.
He has sent me to proclaim release to the captives
and recovering of sight to the blind,
to set at liberty those who are oppressed,
to proclaim the acceptable year of the Lord.
    —Luke 4:18-19

He told his disciples that those who gave food to the hungry, drink to the thirsty, welcomed the stranger, clothed the naked, visited the sick and those in prison, even the least one would be credited as having done it to him and would have a place in glory at the right hand of God (Matthew 25:31-40).

He sent disciples out to preach the gospel, heal the sick, and cast out demons. Under his direction his disciples gathered up food and fed the hungry. No age limit was set.

In a passage from the second letter to the Corinthians, a passage that scholars have designated as the basic Christian message, Paul writes: "Therefore, if any one is in Christ, he is a new creation; the old has passed away, behold, the new has come. All this is from God, who through Christ reconciled us to himself and *gave us the ministry of reconciliation*" (2 Corinthians 5:17-18, emphasis added). Each of us was ordained to ministry at our baptism as a member of a community called to carry out God's purpose.

First Peter 2:9 states, "You are a chosen race, a royal priesthood, a holy nation, God's own people, that you may declare the wonderful deeds of him who called you out of darkness into his marvelous light."

17

The Church's Unique Role in Volunteering

The concepts of mission and commitment to a way of life in which love of God is evidenced by love of the neighbor are the stimuli to philanthropy and social justice.

The philanthropic impulse may not be entirely unique to the Judeo-Christian tradition, but it is deeply rooted there. Most of the ancient civilizations showed little concern for anyone outside the immediate family. In ancient Judaism, however, the concern for justice and for righteousness fostered an ethical outlook which included the whole community. Micah said,

> "With what shall I come before the LORD,
>   and bow myself before God on high? . . ."
> He has showed you, O man, what is good;
>   and what does the LORD require of you
> but to do justice, and to love kindness,
>   and to walk humbly with your God?
>   —Micah 6:6-8

In the Book of Deuteronomy the Hebrews are enjoined:

> At the end of every three years you shall bring forth all the tithe of your produce in the same year, and lay it up within your towns; and the Levite, because he has no portion or inheritance with you, and the sojourner, the fatherless, and the widow, who are within your towns, shall come and eat and be filled; that the LORD your God may bless you in all the work of your hands that you do (Deuteronomy 14:28-29).

In the New Testament Jesus confirmed that all the Law could be summed up in the two great commandments: love God with all your being and love your neighbor as yourself. The writer of the epistles of John declared that one who claims to love God and hates the neighbor is a liar. In the early years of the Christian movement, in keeping with this tradition, the believers developed institutions for taking care of the poor, the sick, and the needy. Early Christian congregations, organized along the lines of the Jewish synagogue, became centers not only for worship but also for charitable responsibility. In the Middle Ages the church, through its orders and monasteries, provided institutions for teaching, healing, and caring for the widow and the orphan.

The European Pietistic movement of the eighteenth century strengthened the concern of church groups to be directly involved in the care of the needy and in social reform. It led to the organization of schools, hospitals, and orphanages. Many of the pietistic groups migrated to the United States since they tended to be dissenters from the established churches. Many of our present institutions, such as universities, hospitals, and social agencies, come from this movement. Under this impetus the evils of slavery, prison, and child labor were fought, and the effort to alleviate them was begun.

Beyond being the source and sanction of the human concern which underlies social welfare programs in general, the church is unique among institutions in the extent to which it is meant to be concerned for the whole person, since its primary function is to clarify the meaning of life in Christian perspective and foster the values, behaviors, and relationship which reflect Jesus' love for all persons. It is not enough to feed, clothe, entertain, and educate. Everyone needs to achieve a point of view, live by a system of values, and cultivate behaviors which are congruent with Christian commitment and faith. One of the values that grows with age is desire for congruence, for life to feel whole, harmonious, and worthwhile, in keeping with one's deepest loves. Therefore, it can be devastating when not only society but also the source of one's nurture, the church, makes it clear that "you are too old now to be a contributing person among us."

The church has a unique function to be a support community, to keep open paths for everyone to do all that is possible to share God's love in the world, to alleviate suffering, to bring joy, and to seek to guide society's structures in accordance with Christian values and the teaching of the Bible.

What Is Volunteering?

1. *Volunteering is citizens working together to create and sustain community*. From the very beginning of our country, many of the settlers came together in groups with the intention of forming communities to help people do together what they could not do alone. The members of these groups were volunteers. They found themselves in a strange new environment and had to pool their efforts to survive.

Today, all over the country, small towns and villages depend upon volunteer fire companies. Most of them have volunteer mayors, city councilmen or selectmen, and volunteer school board members. Even in a city as large as Kansas City, Missouri, which has a paid mayor, city manager, and salaried council members, there are fifty-two boards and committees of volunteers to help shape policy, plan programs, and advise legislative groups and administrative staffs.

2. *Volunteering is concerned persons working together to change social structures and cultural patterns* which exploit, oppress, or retard some for the aggrandizement of others. The abolition of slavery, the franchise of women, the civil rights movement, the labor movement, and the current struggle for equality for women all have derived their impetus and their power from the work of volunteers. The Grey Panthers movement and the National Council of Senior Citizens are made up of volunteers committed to justice for the elderly.

3. *Volunteering is neighbors helping one another* because of mutual concern and because to work together is so much more heartening than to work alone. In nonurban societies generally, families living adjacent to each other developed ties of friendship and patterns of mutual helpfulness. When I lived in a Vermont village in the 1940s, if one was sick, the neighbors would bring in food and offer to run errands. A number of older people spontaneously developed the practice of calling each other to see if they were all right.

But today in urban societies, where persons are more transient, the network of relationships is not determined by geography. Neighborhood awareness has eroded so that neighborly cooperation has to be organized deliberately. *Volunteering is being intentional about the formation of a community or group in which we may express our mutual concern.*

4. *Volunteering is family members providing support for one another* out of love and a sense of responsibility for one another. We live in a time when the character of the family has changed, with fewer children and more adults, with many persons being separated from kinfolk by distance and time. In such a time we need to find or to create *familylike support systems*. We need these systems to help us celebrate our high moments, to comfort us when we are hard pressed, to sustain us when we falter, to assist us when we are disabled. The billions of dollars spent for the care of the sick and the disabled in the United States are far outweighed by the time and money spent by family members voluntarily caring for one another.

5. *Volunteering is the joyous investment of discretionary time in rewarding activity.* It is a means of self-expression even while instrumental to the welfare of others. It is a way in which persons exercise and sharpen their talents as they continue to grow as persons by putting their abilities to use. The phenomenon comes to mind of thousands of men and women regularly studying, planning, learning, and growing as they teach church school classes of all ages, help lagging school children learn to read, read to the blind and the sick, visit the lonely, care for the grieving. Volunteering is a way of expressing gratitude and appreciation for what one has received from God and the community. For those of us committed to the Judeo-Christian tradition and system of values, it is one of the ways we glorify God, live out the love of neighbor, and find meaning in our lives.

The Importance of Volunteers in America

Voluntarism is fundamental in America; it has shaped our way of life and expressed the basic democratic principle that everyone has something to contribute and has the right to contribute it to the good of the whole. Voluntarism is not the privilege of only the elite. It has been estimated that somewhere around forty to fifty million Americans are engaged in volunteer services through some six to seven million voluntary organizations, clubs, churches, causes, and political parties which would not exist except for the time, energy, and money freely poured into them by members who believe in them and see benefit in supporting them.[1] In some of the socialist countries where the government is depended upon to provide for people, voluntary activity and services are unknown.

Trends in Volunteering

In their book *The Volunteer Community: Creative Use of Human Resources* Eva Schindler-Rainman and Ronald Lippitt discuss the trends they see in contemporary society and the implications for voluntarism.[2]

1. The increasing rate and complexity of social and technological change, with the temptation to rely on experts, must be counteracted by volunteers who contribute sensitivity, perspective, and value judgments in dealing creatively with and planning for change.

2. The separation and polarization of social, economic, and political groups require volunteers, along with professionals and paraprofessionals,

to become skillful in taking the third party role in conflict resolution, particularly as more volunteers engage in social action groups.

3. The search for personal meaning, identity, self-renewal, and interpersonal connection demand increasing numbers of volunteers to take leadership in expanding programs of self-study and relationship development and to work with professionals in the helping fields.

4. The changing nature and meaning of work, achievement, leisure, and consumption mean there will be a vast amount of new discretionary time and an increase in the desire for human services.

5. Increase in human service jobs will result in delivery-of-service teams made up of volunteers, paraprofessionals, and professionals working together.

6. The tendency for youth to take over the direction of their own education and socialization processes will call for sensitive adults to help link the younger generation to meaningful opportunities for collaboration and involvement in the larger community and to share perspectives.

7. The new concern for conservation of natural resources challenges volunteers to engage in political action projects.

8. The emergence of a world society calls for volunteers to engage in intercultural exchange and dialogue between countries.

One might add here that the trend toward workers holding down two jobs and wives working outside the home as a way to cope with inflation or raise the standard of living reduces time available for volunteer community service by these younger adults; therefore, all the more important becomes the role of the older volunteer.

Volunteering Is for Everyone

It is true that volunteering depends not upon leisure as such, but upon possession of some discretionary time. People who are working on projects around their own homes, doing their own

---

[1] For more information on the nature of voluntarism in the U.S., see *Volunteering, 1979–1980: A Status Report on America's Volunteer Community* (Washington, D.C., and Boulder, Colo.: VOLUNTEER: The National Center for Citizen Involvement, April, 1980).

[2] Eva Schindler-Rainman and Ronald Lippitt, *The Volunteer Community: Creative Use of Human Resources*, 2nd ed. (Fairfax, Va.: NTL Learning Resources Corporation, 1971, 1975), pp. 20-33.

plumbing, carpentry, car repair, housework, child care, and sick care may be too engaged to feel free to volunteer. Sometimes they can be helped to make a contribution at home. We know a grandmother who stays at home with two grandchildren who realized that she could baby-sit for some other children while she looked after her own. A man who is confined at home because his wife cannot be left alone takes part in a telephone reassurance project. He himself gets relief through a retiree who stays with his wife twice a week.

It is true also that freedom to volunteer comes easier to those who have some confidence about their skills or who welcome the chance to get some skills through training and experience in human relations and group life leadership education available to the volunteer. Some families have a tradition of involvement in community affairs, as do various ethnic groups who often have their own benevolent programs. From the Junior League to the back-lot baseball teams to the labor movement, there is evidence that all sorts of persons can and will give time and effort in the service of causes important to them and to those about whom they care.

It is true also that volunteering can cost money. If the work one does requires transportation or membership fees, meals, stamps for letters, or telephoning, then older people on low fixed incomes face a real deterrent to involvement. The payment of expenses or the provision of a supplement to their other income may be needed to free them to give of their time. Funding may have to be sought to make possible the participation of the less affluent.

There also are persons with very little ego strength who think of themselves as having nothing to contribute. They may never have experienced working with other persons and lack the self-confidence needed to volunteer. We met a woman recently, age sixty-eight, who said our invitation to her to volunteer was the first one ever received. She came twelve years ago from a country where volunteering is unknown, and she assumed that her color and broken English would be a barrier. They actually are her strength in the program in which she has become involved. Some people need support through training experiences that give them confidence and skills. In fact, all volunteers have the right to expect support in being equipped to do their share.

Two Organized Volunteer Programs
The Shepherd's Center

In 1972, Dr. Elbert Cole, pastor of Central United Methodist Church, Kansas City, Missouri, initiated The Shepherd's Center for older people. Sponsored by twenty-five churches and synagogues serving a fifteen-square-mile area of Kansas City in which 25 percent of the population are sixty-five and over, the Shepherd's Center involves about six hundred fifty older people as volunteers in twenty-two different programs. Half of these are home-delivered services, such as meals-on-wheels, handyman's service, friendly visitation, telephone reassurance, companion aides, emergency medical transportation, shopper's assistance, and hospice care. Half are center-based programs, such as continuing education, mental health education and human relations training, health screening and health education, employment counseling and job placement, a drop-in center, a day out for persons with handicapping conditions, creative arts, and a forum-type luncheon.

The Shepherd concept of a program for older people, controlled by and delivered by older people themselves, has generated twenty-five to thirty similar centers across the country in inner-city settings, rural settings, and working class neighborhood settings, as well as suburban settings. In 1977, CBS produced a half-hour documentary film on the Shepherd's Center called ''Volunteer to Live.'' In 1978, *Guideposts* magazine gave the Central United Methodist Church of Kansas City the Church of the Year award for its role in starting and supporting the Shepherd's Center.

Project Head

In 1969, when she was serving as program director of the Philadelphia Center for Older People, Mrs. Victorina Peralta initiated a program which came to be known as HEAD (Help Elderly Adults Direct). In her capacity as a volunteer to Catholic Social Services in the archdiocese of Philadelphia, Mrs. Peralta organized the first group (at 4700 Springfield Avenue, Philadelphia) for a project committed to serving the whole person with emphasis upon social experiences, health maintenance, education, cultural opportunities, leisure time activities, and civic action. The older people themselves have taken the primary role in developing, planning, and carrying out programs with the support of priests, rabbis, and pastors.

Within a short time the idea took hold throughout the archdiocese of Philadelphia, with groups meeting in 165 parishes. It has been picked up so that by 1980 there were 36 in Allentown, Pennsylvania, 18 in Erie, Pennsylvania, 60 in Harrisburg, Pennsylvania, 27 in Clearwater, Florida, 55 in Houston, Texas, 40 in Baltimore, Maryland, and others. Thousands of older people have performed significant volunteer service through these clubs. Numerous illustrations of their service are given in the manual *Project Head*.[3]

In Summary

Older people have a primary role to play in the ministry of the church. To be a Christian is by definition to be in ministry. The leadership of the church is challenged to enable its older members to recognize and live out their vocations, giving freely as they have received.

[3]Victorina Peralta, *Project HEAD. Help Elderly Adults Direct.* For information write Director, Adult and Aging Services Division, Department of Public Welfare, 1221 Sansom St., Philadelphia, PA 19107.

WARNING:
YOU CAN BE
REPLACED
BY A
VOLUNTEER

Chapter 3

The Professional and the Volunteer

Before professionals discuss and plan how to recruit and how to work effectively with older volunteers, they need first of all to be sure that they really want to work with volunteers at all, let alone older volunteers. Some professionals would much prefer not to be bothered by volunteers; thus, they work with them reluctantly as a matter of necessity. Until professionals have become clear about their own motives and attitudes toward volunteers, they are going to have difficulty in working with volunteers, no matter what their age.

Why Involve Volunteers at All?

Do you seek volunteers primarily because you have a lot of things to get done and you can't afford to hire help? In that case, you may be tempted to exploit persons to do what others usually get paid for, and they will resent being used in this way. Or will you be using persons as means to your end and thus depersonalizing them? Do you want volunteers to take the dirty work off your hands and do the less interesting and less meaningful tasks around your church or agency so that you can be free to spend all your time

doing the really interesting things? Then you are in danger of trivializing and demeaning the role of the volunteer or of taking the challenge out of volunteering. As long as you see the program as yours rather than as one which is to be a team effort, you will have trouble with volunteers.

In fact, there are those who believe that we cannot count on volunteers for competent and dependable services. Such doubters would professionalize and pay for all human services. Others argue that we cannot depend on volunteer church school teachers any longer to provide quality teaching, and, therefore, we must begin to pay persons so we can demand training and faithfulness to the task. We live in a money economy in which we expect to pay for services we do not perform for ourselves; so why, some argue, should anyone donate competent service to persons outside one's own family?

Some are disillusioned with volunteers. Others see voluntarism as a kind of exploitation, as cheap labor, which deprives others of paid work. The women's movement, minorities, and labor unions have questioned voluntarism as exploitation and unfair competition. The result is a federal regulation by the National Labor Relations Board forbidding a volunteer to do any work ordinarily done by a paid employee.

However, many things need to be done in a community, for which we can never pay without backbreaking pressure on the tax structure or huge contributions of money.

But deeper than that, no free community can long survive unless citizens are willing to give time freely for services that benefit the community. We need responsible participation to identify with the community, all the way from keeping the streets free of litter and the parks and playgrounds clean to holding public office.

As human beings, to become human, we need to share our lives with others. We need to realize that our opportunity for service is opportunity to fulfill our lives if the job we do fits our capabilities and interests and gives us a share in the creation of a community safe and satisfying in which to live.

The Professional's Relation to the Volunteer

Consciously or unconsciously, professionals often distrust and resist making use of volunteers except in the most passive positions and for the most trivial jobs, with little or no authority and ill-defined roles.

People in the helping professions have worked long and hard to develop standards of training and to gain credentials of competence. They have seen too many instances of well-intentioned but insensitive and untrained amateurs. In reaction they may tend to overlook the importance of the supportive, informal networks of family and friends and people who come to help because they care and not because they are paid to serve. It is now becoming clear that the physical, mental, and spiritual health of a person is a community process, not only an individual matter. Therefore, one of the main roles of the professional is to educate and train the volunteer workers to provide

competent, supportive help and effective, healing services. Volunteers, just as professionals, need to be screened, properly assigned, trained, and supervised.

It takes time to recruit, train, delegate, and supervise assistants. However, the only way to multiply and extend the work of a professional is to provide trained volunteer associates to collaborate as a team to carry out a helping program. Therefore, the professional person who works with volunteers needs to respect them and to have enough management and supervisory skills and time to teach, guide, and support volunteers until they become competent colleagues, sharing the work and decision making. The professional is to "model" staff behavior and attitudes.

The development and management of volunteers is now itself a profession, especially important for organizations that depend on volunteer services. Professionals who work with volunteers do well to receive management training. This is especially important for clergy who are the enabling professional ministers in the midst of a community of volunteer ministers.

An issue for both volunteer and professional staff is the power and decision-making issue. Who participates in which decisions and at what level?

Sherry R. Arnstein has developed a helpful typology, "A Ladder of Citizen Participation," to help analyze where an organization stands with respect to citizen volunteer participation. The lowest rung on the ladder is "manipulation." The next is "therapy," the third is "informing," the fourth "consultation," and the fifth "placation." The sixth rung is "partnership," the seventh "delegated power," and the eighth and final rung is "citizen control." One might take exception to the need for therapy to be conducted without the participation of the patient, but in the main this ladder points up the different ways that constituencies are involved.

At the lowest level agencies seek to "educate" or "cure" without any citizen voice. At the middle level, there is some communication and some opportunity to influence decisions from the outside. At the highest level participants are engaged directly in the decision-making process.[1]

Not everyone wants to participate in every decision, nor is everyone so qualified. The range of decision-making possibilities and the kind of process appropriate to each situation need to be understood. The varied degree of participation of professional and volunteer in decision making is illustrated by the chart that follows.

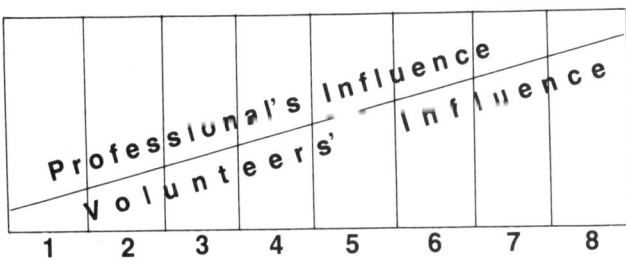

1. The professional decides and tells the volunteers what to do.

2. The professional decides, and then explains and tries to persuade the volunteers to accept his or her judgment.

3. The professional may hear the volunteers' suggestions and then decide for them.

4. The professional consults with the volunteers, then decides what he or she believes the volunteers want.

5. The professional consults with volunteers, then lets them make the decision.

6. The volunteers consult the professional and then make their own decision.

7. The volunteers decide, then cajole, persuade, or pressure the professional to do what they want.

8. The volunteers decide and tell the professional what is to be done.

This chart makes no value judgments about which way is better. As a general rule, however,

persons tend to invest more energy into what they have helped to determine.

Opportunities for Volunteer Service

Many types of organizations need volunteers and count on them. Institutions such as hospitals, museums, and settlement houses have volunteer departments to supplement the work of paid staff. These institutions may be public or private, large or small.

Agencies such as the Red Cross and the Boy Scouts are designed for small staffs and many volunteers. The church is in this category, being a community of volunteers assisted in ministry by the professionally trained.

Finally, there are organizations with no staff at all and yet carry on innumerable activities. These may be clubs, special interest groups, and advocacy groups.

Types of Volunteer Services

In terms of the functional classification of work performed by volunteers, we find the following:

- Services to individuals and families
- Services to children in congregate settings, such as nursery schools and day care centers
- Health organizations, such as hospitals
- Services to elderly in nursing homes
- Recreation, leisure, and education services
- Religious leadership in churches and synagogues
- Research, planning, promotion, making surveys
- Advocacy and ombudsmanship
- Office services
- Production, distribution, and repair
- Specialist services—using vocational training
- Neighborhood self-help, mutual help services as part of informal network

[1]Sherry R. Arnstein, "A Ladder of Citizen Participation," *Journal of the American Institute of Planners*, vol. 35, no. 4 (July, 1969), pp. 216-224.

Types of Volunteer Roles

Another kind of classification sorts volunteer jobs according to the kind of activity involved:

- *Administrative:* organizing, staffing, coordinating, planning
- *Direct service:* visiting, teaching, leading games, delivering meals to homes, home repairs, health delivery services
- *Indirect service:* office work, library, research, information and referral, making cookies
- *Policy making:* serving on boards
- *Fund raising:* canvassing, letter writing, earning money
- *Advocacy:* making presentations, agitating, ombudsmanship
- *Consultation:* sharing knowledge and experience in conversation

The Factor of Remuneration

Another way of looking at volunteering is through the lens of remuneration. The variations are:

- The volunteer who receives no pay and who also may pay his or her expenses.
- The volunteer whose expenses are paid and who, in addition, may receive supplemental remuneration, such as free lunches, trips to conferences, and uniforms. In fact, the payment of expenses may be necessary for persons on small pensions to participate.
- The volunteer who may be spending full-time on the job but is willing and able to do it for a small stipend or subsistence reimbursement, such as board and room. Older people sometimes volunteer for such work to supplement pensions or gain a little additional income. Because they have pensions and are free of heavy responsibilities for the support of others, older people have been able to volunteer for service as missionaries or workers in poverty-stricken communities.

The Sponsorship of Volunteer Services

Volunteering has its roots in spontaneous and generous acts of neighborliness. In the small, well-established community, volunteer neighborliness may just happen. Residents may work out signals which indicate to other neighbors that they are all right, such as lifting a particular window shade to a certain height in the morning. Friends may get into the routine of calling one another at certain times, just to be sure the other is all right. When one gets sick, others may take in casseroles and do such things as clean up the kitchen. Persons who drive may run errands for those not able to go out themselves. Groups often take up collections of money, clothing, and household supplies to help one who has had a fire. A retired mailman, handy with tools, does odd jobs for elderly people in his neighborhood.

In the urban community, while such spontaneous acts of volunteer service do occur quite frequently, it still is necessary to be deliberate about organizing the community to plan for neighborliness. Existing organizations, such as churches, Granges, and lodges may take the lead in organizing these services. In some high-crime areas the police are organizing volunteers to participate in what is known as Neighborhood Watch, an intergenerational project in which young children and older folk are proving to be key participants. Circles, classes, and clubs may generate volunteer programs. Special groups to meet special needs may be formed.

Various types of community planning councils and community centers may assume responsibility for organizing volunteer services. The multipurpose comprehensive senior center which plans programs for the older people within a given service delivery area is one of the newest kinds of community agencies for the design and coordination of services. Such centers began in the late 1940s but did not burgeon until the 1970s. The new guidelines of the 1978 amendments to the Older Americans Act encourage the development of a comprehensive, coordinated continuum of services for older people in every community—a new kind of community institution.

Specific Volunteer Services

The kinds of services older volunteers can be responsible for are endless and as varied as imagination can conceive. They fall into three major headings.

Services Provided to Persons in Their Homes

Friendly visiting
Telephone reassurance
Counseling, support, and need assessment
Meals on wheels
Shopping assistance
Transportation to medical services
Emergency hotline
Handyman
Visiting nurse
Crime protection assistance
Hospice support
Reading, writing letters

Services Provided at Centers

Teaching and tutoring
Leading recreation and playground supervision
Supervising crafts and recreation

Serving at health clinics and fairs
Rendering income-tax assistance
Legal aid
Receptionist, host, office worker
Planning parties
Helping to cook and serve meals
Organizing tours and expeditions
Helping with day care, mother's day out
Consulting on business management
Working in employment service
Developing public relations
Information and referral

Services Out and About

Raising money
Speaking
Serving on committees
Community block watch activities
Foster parent and foster grandparent activities

In Summary

Professionals and their skills and services are essential in every community.

But innumerable human needs are met by volunteers, and rightly so. The society cannot pay for all that needs to be done. Although we read of large sums being allocated by government agencies, 80 percent of older persons' care is supplied by family and friends and 20 percent through public funding.

Chapter 4

Motivating Volunteers to Serve

In a basic sense we cannot motivate persons to volunteer or to act in any particular way if by "motivate persons" we mean to persuade them to do what they do not want to do or whatever the motivator wants them to do. Rather, we appeal to motives already present. We do that by offering persons opportunities to meet their basic needs, to actualize the values to which they are committed, and to spend their energies in gratifying ways.

We can help persons understand their needs, clarify their values, and evaluate activities that may be satisfying. We can share visions of possibilities. We can stimulate imagination about desirable things that could be. We can touch the springs of human action. But we cannot motivate one who does not want to be motivated.

Ways of Looking at Motives

Those persons who live with intentionality in the stream of Judeo-Christian consciousness may have stirring within them words read by Jesus from the book of the prophet Isaiah:

The Spirit of the Lord is upon me,
because he has anointed me to preach good news to
the poor.

He has sent me to proclaim release to the captives
and recovering of sight to the blind,
to set at liberty those who are oppressed,
to proclaim the acceptable year of the Lord.
—Luke 4:18-19

Such echoes, coupled with the great commandments to love God with all our heart and soul and mind and to love our neighbor as ourselves do raise yearnings in some people for ways and means to give loving service in response to the "call of everyman." Does this sensitivity come from recognizing ourselves on the threshold of the needy? Does it come from the stirring of the Spirit? As human beings we are energized in various ways.

We may look at motivation of the volunteer from three different perspectives. One focuses upon the rewards in relation to the costs. A second analyzes the forces for volunteering which are in tension with the forces against volunteering. The third examines the attractiveness of the behavioral setting to the volunteer and the ease of entry or freedom from barriers. The implication of the first is that we need to enhance the incentives to volunteering. The implication of the second is that we need to reduce the inhibiting forces. The implication of the third is that we need to make the setting both attractive and easy to enter.

1. Enhance the Incentives

As volunteers, all of us consider the costs as well as the rewards. We ask ourselves, in effect, if being a volunteer is worth the cost. The cost— or investment, if you prefer—is the time, the energy, and in some cases the money the volunteer would be expected to contribute that might otherwise be invested in another activity. An investment always entails some risk. The activity may not pay off. It may lead to unforeseen complications. It may result in pain, embarrassment, or loss. So we weigh the risk as well as the cost and the reward.

The reward is the satisfaction we get from service rendered, such as the appreciation of those receiving the service, the thrill of accomplishment, the satisfaction of having adequate resources, the recognition from peers, the companionship experienced, friendships made in the course of the activity, and the good feeling that comes from a congruence between caring feelings and caring actions. Some of us discover that by doing loving deeds for others, our own depressions and loneliness are dispelled. Rewards come in many ways, but unless the reward outweighs the cost, we are not likely to volunteer or to continue in a volunteer activity.

What rewards can we offer to volunteers for giving their time and energy to the service of others? Various studies cast light upon the rewards.

We all like to do what is significant and important. We want to believe that what we are doing will make a difference in directions we value. Therefore, we need to lay before potential volunteers the significance of what they are asked to become involved in and how important their service will be to the success of the total enterprise.

We all like to be involved with those whom we like personally and whom we admire. The fellowship that comes from working with others is often named as one of the most rewarding aspects of volunteer service. Therefore, we need to establish warm, friendly, personal relationships with potential volunteers. We need to make them feel welcomed and wanted as part of the fellowship. We need to hold out to them the joy of being a part of a ministering community without glossing over the challenges which can occur in any set of relationships.

We all like to do those things which stimulate us to grow and to develop as persons. In many cases, with the young, with the person returning to the labor market, and with older people looking for new careers, volunteer service can be the way of entry into a new occupation. But in any case the training and experience gained can be held up as opportunities to become better informed, better adjusted to life, and more broadly oriented as a person.

In a struggling church school of a small church, the young pastor was dismayed when a woman who was one of the best trained and most effective teachers resigned because she had decided "to go through the chairs in Eastern Star," and this would demand all of her free time. Obviously she found her involvement in Eastern Star lodge more significant and more rewarding than her work in the church. The lodge had more status in that community. Her best friends were active there. She would be accorded much recognition as she advanced from one rank to another.

2. Reduce the Inhibiting Forces

Another way of understanding the motivation of volunteers is to conceive of the volunteer as a field of forces in tension with one another, with some forces encouraging commitment to volunteer service and other forces working against involvement. We might conceive of this as internal voices arguing with one another.

In the book *The Volunteer Community: Cre-*

ative Use of Human Resources the authors provide a graphic way of looking at the conflicting forces.[1] They see these forces operative within the volunteer, within the context of the volunteer's interactions with others, and within the situation. We may experience these conflicting forces as if they were inner voices arguing with one another within us.

For example, in terms of our own feelings about ourselves and our situations, we might hear some of the following dialogues as we try to reach a decision:

Yes	No
I need something to do and I want to spend my time doing something really interesting.	If I did that, it would tie me down so that I could do nothing else.
It would meet a critical need, and I want to do my part.	It's controversial and I might get involved in conflict.
It is very challenging and would be an important job.	I'm not sure I have the skill and experience needed to do it.

In terms of the interpersonal and group member forces, we might find conflicts such as these:

Yes	No
My best friends are involved.	My family wants me to spend more time with them.
Some skilled and well-known people are involved, and I would get to work with them.	My family and friends would make fun of me.

[1]For the source on which the following examples of conflicting forces are based, see Eva Schindler-Rainman and Ronald Lippitt, *The Volunteer Community: Creative Use of Human Resources,* 2nd ed. (Fairfax, Va.: NTL Learning Resources Corporation, 1971, 1975), pp. 48-49.

Yes	No
Service is a part of the tradition in my family.	Other people are getting paid to do that kind of work.

In terms of the forces governing the situation, these kinds of tensions may be encountered:

Yes	No
It would be an interesting place to work.	Transportation would be a real problem.
Our national leaders are urging us to get involved in this.	I would have to go into an area where there is a lot of crime.

This list could continue on and on. Just as there are conflicting forces encountered in making the decision to be a volunteer, so there are forces operative encouraging us to continue and pressing us to drop out. Of course these forces work differently in different persons and the forces are not always of the same strength.

Schindler-Rainmann and Lippitt summarized their findings in this way:[2]

Reasons for Responding to a Plea for Participation

1. Some persons responded to *possibilities for self-actualization, others to opportunities for service, duty, and the repayment of a "service rendered."*

2. Some were *inner-oriented*—relying upon their own feelings, their own sense of relevance, their own values as guidelines for the decision to respond; others were *other-oriented*—influenced by the norms of the group, by potential visibility and status, by potentialities for job and social relationships.

3. Some persons were interested in *action,* others in *reflection and policy.*

4. Some were interested in *power and influence;* others were primarily interested in the op-

[2]Schindler-Rainman and Lippitt, *op. cit.,* pp. 50-56.

portunities for *emotional associations with others*.

5. Some persons identified with the *larger community* and its welfare; others were oriented toward the *interpersonal and group membership meanings* of the particular opportunity. The latter were interested in the image of the people they would be working with, the type of interpersonal support they would receive, and the meaning this activity would have for friends, family, and other groups to which they belong.

6. Some were *autonomy-oriented,* some were *interdependence-oriented,* and others were *dependence- or support-oriented*. The first looked forward to the freedom to take some risks, try new ways, and find new excitement. The second prized mutual, collegial support from peers and working relationships, while the third were concerned about a clearly defined job, arrangements for training, and on-the-job supervision and help.

Reasons for Dropping Out

1. *Unreal expectations* built up in the recruiting process.

2. *Lack of appreciative feedback* from co-workers and staff.

3. *Lack of consultative support* from the staff.

Reasons for Continuing in Service
(besides initial reasons for joining)

1. The *sense of "making a difference,"* of contributing to some meaningful service that changes or helps the lives of others.

2. The *sense of self-actualization,* of feeling more competent, learning much, seeing the possibility of transferring the learnings to other phases of life.

There is always the temptation to try to move persons by stepping up the pressure to volunteer, by emphasizing the desirability of saying yes, by being persuasive and giving all the reasons why one should, by appealing to a sense of duty, by raising feelings of guilt for refusing, by threatening consequences if they do not volunteer. In most cases the increasing pressure succeeds in raising the level of the inhibiting forces and causes the potential volunteer to draw on the defenses of rationalization, evasion, halfhearted assent, or a host of excuses. The better strategy is to take the inhibiting factors seriously, deal with them as they become apparent, and attempt to work with the person to reduce them by positive programs, to change the balance of forces within the person, within the social environment, or within the situation.

Providing transportation, paying expenses, working in teams, changing the schedule—all are ways of reducing inhibiting forces.

3. Make the Behavioral Settings Attractive and Easy to Enter

A third way of thinking about the motivation of volunteers is to conceive of the organization as a behavioral setting. A behavioral setting is made up of physical objects, places, and persons. Within each behavioral setting there are activities and behaviors which are considered appropriate and expected. Such settings tend to be composed of particular kinds of persons; other persons would not be expected there.

A behavioral setting can be thought of as made up of a series of concentric circles. The outer circle represents the least amount of involvement in the setting, the inner circle the most. As a person enters the setting, she or he has minimal involvement. As her or his participation becomes more intense and wholehearted, she or he penetrates to a central position in the setting. This is illustrated by the figure on page 33.

Some settings are attractive and easy to enter. Others are forbidding and exclusive. In some settings the persons found there are interesting, warm, and friendly. In others they seem cold, disinterested, and even dull. Some buildings and offices seem to say, "Walk in. Make yourself at home. We have a good time here." Other buildings and offices seem to say, "Only the initiated

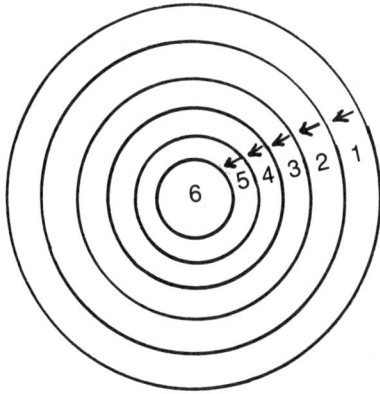

1. Onlooker: resident in parish
2. Casual attender: comes into building
3. Participates in program
4. Becomes a worker/volunteer
5. Becomes a decision maker/ officer
6. Made a staff member

can enter here. Watch your step. Don't cause any trouble. You are in our way.'' Look at some of the following physical features to see how attractive your setting is:

- The entrance is visible, easily identified, marked.
- Access is easy with a ramp, no steps, and ample light.
- Parking and loading space are available and easily found.
- The decor is imaginative and the colors are warm.
- The furniture is attractive and invitingly arranged.
- Offices and desks are approachable.

Settings can be made inviting in terms of personal behavior also. Check out the positive values of the following:

- Receptionists meet persons coming in. They are friendly, interested, and helpful.
- Persons are met by the staff or leaders with warm greetings. There is time for them.
- The staff shows interest in getting to know people and to be of use to them.
- Newcomers are accepted quickly as members and are appointed to committees and offices.

Attitudes and Predispositions Toward Volunteering

Some persons are drawn to volunteer service. If they are free, they gladly accept invitations to become involved. If not approached first, they may even actively seek out opportunities to get involved. Others, however, seem to shy away from participation in social activities, shun opportunities to take responsibility or leadership, and avoid making commitments. Some turn to the church to find avenues of self-expression, while others avoid the church but look for involvement or accept involvement in other organizations.

These patterns of personal behavior may be lifetime characteristics. These patterns reflect attitudes and values learned through experience with persons, situations, and activities. Every experience is accompanied by pain or pleasure, by satisfaction or frustration. These give rise to tendencies to repeat the experience or to avoid it. So one develops predispositions to respond favorably or unfavorably, positively or negatively, in regard to specific persons, situations, and activities.

For example, a child who goes to school and from the beginning experiences only failure and frustration will develop a negative attitude toward school. If the child is a member of a social group which belittles schooling or which belittles the child's capacity to learn, the child will have a negative attitude toward school from the start.

Predispositions to respond negatively or positively toward specific objects are known as attitudes. If these tendencies are widely generalized and even abstracted into ideas of what is desirable, they are known as values. Thus one may come to value intellectual learning as an end in itself. Values are usually laid down early in life and reinforced by the expectancies of the groups to which one belongs and upon which one depends.

These attitudes tend to be tied up with images of the self as a particular kind of person, and these images in turn are reinforced by the expectations of those with whom one associates. So attitudes not only are learned by one's own experience, but also they are supported and reinforced by social groups. One may take on the attitudes of the group to which one belongs, or one may seek out a group that is sympathetic to certain attitudes. Finally, these attitudes become a part of one's own ego identity.

Attitudes and values can be changed by the introduction of new and different experiences. They can be changed by becoming a member of a group that has a different attitude. However, attitudes usually change slowly and with great difficulty. They are easiest to change if they are not deeply imprinted, if they are not a part of the social norms of the group with which a person is identified, or if they do not demand a revolution in one's way of thinking about oneself.

In working with older volunteers, we are dealing with persons who have a lifetime of experience behind them to deepen attitudes. Some of them look forward to retirement just so they can give more time to volunteer activities. When they retire, they plan to find something to do and expect to look for it by volunteer service in a community organization. Some older people, however, have had little or no experience in volunteering. They may never have been asked. They may have been too mobile or too busy to get involved. They may have resisted involvement because of the attitudes they have toward themselves and others.

If they do not have negative attitudes toward volunteering, we may be able to find ways to involve them, beginning with the things they know how to do and through training helping them to learn new things. If, however, they have negative attitudes toward involvement with others, toward altruistic activity, toward their own capacity, and if they are "loners," it may be extremely difficult or even impossible.

To counter such conditioning, a process of several steps may be needed. We will have to establish a relationship of trust with these persons so that they can at least relate to one person and begin to identify with that person. Then we may have to entice them to do minor things which they can do by themselves. Next, we will try to broaden their range of social relationships and try to draw them into some kind of group membership. At that point they may be able to join with the group in some kind of volunteer activity.

Many older people have been made to believe that retirement is a time to withdraw, to sit and do nothing. They may even be persuaded by children of friends or persons in the community to become "disengaged" and to take the role of "an old man" or "old woman," to "take it easy." People stop asking them for help. If they are asked, they feel helpless and unable because they have incorporated the negative stereotype of later maturity.

The involvement or reengagement of such persons starts with holding up images of possibility to them and to those who pressure them. The director of a day care center for older persons with handicapping conditions admitted an elderly gentleman who had become completely uncommunicative, uncooperative, and apathetic. Within a couple of weeks he began to talk, to laugh, and to enter into social activities as he saw others participating and as the staff expected him to do.

Some might say that volunteers ought to serve in the same spirit in which we dance or write poetry or sing, that service is not an instrumental activity we perform for a reward but an emotional-expressive role we take because it is our nature to love just as much as it is to sing. Volunteering can take on some of the characteristics of writing poetry or dancing as being inherently satisfying in itself. Therefore, we need not be concerned for recognition, appreciation, or response. However, if the impulse to sing or dance is met with indifference or disapproval, it is soon extinguished.

Others tend to urge volunteer service as a

Christian duty to be done, not because we like to do it or want to do it, but because it is commanded—done to avoid punishment in the hereafter or perhaps to gain a star in our crown in the great beyond. But in our time particularly, appeals to a sense of duty are ineffective, for if volunteering is done grudgingly at the command of conscience, it is likely to be an unhappy experience that will communicate itself to those we serve. Volunteer service must be seen as rewarding. As Jesus himself said, "I came that they may have life, and have it abundantly" (John 10:10).

Volunteering Functions Best in a Climate of Shared Leadership

Many organizations which complain about not being able to secure volunteers unconsciously or inadvertently fend off volunteers because they are unwilling to share power, authority, or the limelight with them. Oligarchies and close circles insure that persons outside will not be available for volunteer services. In such groups only the menial, trivial tasks are available for volunteers, and persons with ability who are looking for challenging tasks cannot get into the group.

A pastor, appointed to a church of eighteen hundred members, soon discovered that about ten persons held every significant office in the church. He realized that unless that church broadened its base of leadership, in a few years it would be bereft not only of leaders but also of participants. When he had opportunity to hire an associate, he opted to take on a lay person trained in personnel management. This person surveyed the membership to discover what talents persons possessed and then developed a file from which information could be quickly retrieved. For example, the pastor asked the personnel director if there were any members of the church who could direct a religious drama. Within twenty minutes he came in and laid the names of six persons on the pastor's desk. As a result of this concern for securing wide participation, this church found a way to tap the potential of its members in ways that not only strengthened the church but also contributed to the growth of the persons involved.

In developing a climate for voluntarism, it is important to work at building a community where persons care about one another and begin to assume mutual reponsibility with and for one another. In this the pastor or other leaders set the pace by exhibiting these characteristics in their own behavior and through the covenants that persons have with one another.

Building a climate of shared leadership begins in the nursery and kindergarten of the church school and continues all the way through. Everything that is done to encourage and train and give practice in taking leadership at any age is a contribution to the climate and a way of building a reservoir of competent, participating members. The child who takes responsibility for putting away toys, for cleaning the chalkboard, or for bringing in a brief report is being prepared for leadership on a larger scale.

Vocational Counseling

For youth and young adults there needs to be a program of vocational counseling to help persons become aware of and attentive to their calling. This takes the form of individual and small group conferences in which persons are helped to make decisions about what they want to do with their lives and what they must do to prepare themselves for what they choose. In addition to the choice of occupations, there will be decisions about relationships to the community and to other persons.

Life-planning courses and seminars for adults can make important contributions to a climate of responsible member participation. As persons clarify their values, learn what they feel fulfilled in doing, set goals for their own fulfillment, they are clarifying relationships with others and with community organizations. Life planning may involve not only interviews, discussion, and reading but also exploration, through field trips, of the kinds of things persons do.

Preretirement planning programs represent another aspect of life planning for persons who are approaching the later years and facing the prospect of mandatory retirement or the question of whether to retire when there is no required time to do so. This may be coupled with retirement counseling for those who are on the verge and are making the transition to retirement.

The principle that one does not retire *from* but *to* something is sound. For most persons, satisfaction in retirement stems from becoming involved in activities which use the skills they have acquired and providing opportunity to grow by developing new skills. This kind of involvement can structure time, provide identifiable status in the community, give significance to life, and open opportunities for fellowship with others.

Those who have been loners and socially uninvolved most of their lives may not present themselves for vocational counseling. But if they do, there may be things they can do in keeping with their life-style that enable them to praise God and love the neighbor.

The call to Christian ministry comes through the discovery of what one can do and enjoys doing. It comes through awareness of the needs of others which one may be in a position to meet, and of needs which one has that can be met through service. It comes in the opening of op-portunities for activity and creation as well as in the closing of some doors. Each person must learn to listen and to hear what talent, need, and opportunity say. Then each person's perception of calling must be tested and confirmed both by experience and by the prayerful judgments of the congregation. Ultimately God's call to ministry is mediated through the ministering community in terms of the nurture it provides, the challenges it presents, and the opportunities it makes available.

In Summary

Volunteers will say yes—if
- you offer them a significant, challenging, and rewarding role.
- they are able to do the task successfully.
- they anticipate a warm welcome and friendship from fellow workers.
- you support them with equipment, training, and personal presence.
- they believe in the goals and purpose of the project.

Volunteers will stay with it—if
- they continue to be able to do it.
- they are needed, recognized, appreciated, and patted on the back.
- they find themselves growing as persons.
- they enjoy what they are doing and the persons with whom they are working.

Managing
Volunteer Ministries with
Older People

We now turn to a consideration of specific processes and techniques involved in working with older volunteers. These are presented step by step in the order in which they appropriately are faced. However, you may want to turn to a specific chapter that meets your immediate need for information and suggestions about how to proceed or how to solve a pressing problem.

Chapter 5

Set the Stage for Ministry

When we become a member of the church, we do two things: (1) We put ourselves in the midst of a community where we may be enabled to grow as a person, be supported in time of stress, and be confirmed in a way which leads to life eternal; (2) we commit ourselves to be a part of the ministry of that community, both the ministry of members one to another and the ministry of the congregation to the world. Ministry is an integral part of the way to life eternal and of the way through which we grow as persons.

Becoming a member of the Christian community is a voluntary decision. It also implies that we plan to volunteer money and time to the church's ministry. The understanding of the nature of the Christian community and of our commitment is basic to the involvement of volunteers.

Clarify the Mission of the Congregation

To be clear about the nature and mission of the church is step one for ministry. General clarification of purpose takes place in services of worship, in Scripture study and prayers, through hymns of praise and commitment, and as sermons are preached and church history is recalled. Unfortunately, generalizations are seldom motivating.

Specific clarity about mission needs to be achieved in intentional planning conferences: "Why does this church exist? How does this congregation and how do I as a member of this congregation take part in God's plan for the redemption of the world, *in this place?* How do we, and specifically I, love God and neighbor as ourselves *here?* Who are my neighbors?" What are they to me and I to them? And if we do relate, how does this congregation relate to us? Energy for mission can be released, and vision clarified, as Christians struggle together for answers to such questions as these.[1]

Determine the Needs

The second step is to determine to which persons and needs a response is to be made. How can this be done?

[1] See Richard E. Rusbuldt, Richard K. Gladden, and Norman M. Green, Jr., *Local Church Planning Manual* (Valley Forge: Judson Press, 1977), for guidance in clarifying the mission of the church and subsequent steps in the planning process.

39

1. Gather a Concerned and Representative Group to Share What Its Members Know from Experience

Think about what human beings need, what you need to be human, to become who you can be—are such needs being met where you live, within range of your church? Are the people you are talking about represented in your group? Mission is best defined when the constituency to be served can somehow participate, be represented, in the planning.

2. Listen to the Cries of Those Who Hurt

If persons are asked directly what they need, they may say they do not need anything or that they can get along all right as is. They are reluctant to admit needs for fear of embarrassment or rejection, having been taught through the years that they should stand on their own feet and work things out themselves. Or people may give up ever satisfying their needs and in despair deny them. Some have denied their needs so long they no longer know their needs, let alone their desires, and are unable to articulate what they feel. Some have forgotten to listen to what their bodies and souls say to them.

These cries, whether voiced or not, need to be heard by pastorally minded, sensitive persons who listen and observe, who may have been through similar experiences themselves and know what deprivation and despair can do to people. *Caring* is the issue here.

3. Conduct Systematic Surveys

Bishop Francis J. McConnell of the Methodist church said that to be Christian is to read statistics with compassion. Statistics, developed competently through carefully designed data collection, can say much that needs to be known about community needs. Census data, data compiled by planning commissions, research projects done by universities, and various research agen-

cies can be valuable for need determination.

The planning process can be more sharply focused, however, if the persons themselves who are in our constituency are asked what their situation is and what kind of response they would welcome. In planning, it is important to listen and observe. The nuances and overtones and hints may be as important as the objective data gained by direct inquiry.

4. Be Open to New Visions of Possibility

Many times congregations want to "do something for" particular groups of individuals or want to deal with specific problems but flounder as they try to comprehend responsibly. Read, visit other sites, confer with agencies, participate in training programs to discover what has been and can be done.

5. Offer Pilot Programs to Test Needs

Once they infer that a need may exist, sometimes the only way to find out if it really does is to experiment with a program to test the need. As the colloquialism puts it, "Run up a flag and see if anyone salutes it." This may be an expensive and even a disappointing way to learn, but it may be necessary. If a pilot program does not work, it is always important to ask if this means there is no need, if the idea was before its time, or if the program was not well conceived.

6. Select Priority Needs

Any survey of needs is likely to uncover more needs than any group can hope to meet. Ministry starts with a decision about needs which have priority. In addition to the crucial character of the need, a priority has to be selected upon the basis of being able to do something about it. *A group starts by doing those things which they have the resources to do at that time.*

7. Set Objectives for Ministry

Once a need has been uncovered, determine

the objective: describe the state you want to create as a result of your activity. Objectives are most useful when measurable so that after a determined length of time one can say what has been done and what the action has accomplished. An illustration of an objective is the following: By the end of the year every homebound person will have been visited each month.

Describe the Tasks Essential to Achieve Objectives

Needs are met by persons who do specific things. Ministries succeed when persons are organized effectively to coordinate all the specific tasks.

1. Analyze the Specific Tasks Needed

After the setting of objectives, the next step is to make a list of all the activities and tasks which must be done to reach the objective. It is helpful to arrange these tasks in the order in which they must be done.

An astute business manager became the superintendent of a large Sunday church school. The first thing he did was simply to observe, getting acquainted with all that went on. As he did so, he noticed things that no one was doing. He saw that new families came almost every Sunday to enter a member in a class, but when the family members came in the door, they were lost and bewildered because there was no person and no sign to direct them. He suggested the need for a receptionist with a desk near the door and some ushers to be available to guide persons through the building. He also saw that when the curriculum materials arrived, he sorted them and got them to the teachers. He suggested a curriculum librarian and the use of the ushers to deliver curriculum. He saw that there were a number of communications to get out each week. He found a secretary who volunteered to make such dispatching her contribution to the work of the church school.

In order to test further the list of tasks to be done, one can ask, "What would happen if no one did any of these? Would it make any difference?" Tasks we are going to ask volunteers to perform must be essential to the person involved. They also must support the values to which we are committed as Christians.

Clarity about the task is essential for motivation and recruitment of volunteers and later for evaluation of their work.

2. Write Out Job Descriptions

To avoid misunderstandings and to be specific about the work to be done, write a job description.

A job description lists expectations, when the job begins and ends, the time required, training available, the job supervisor, and available support. A prospective volunteer may wish to suggest a change in the job description in order to fit his or her situation more responsibly.

See the examples of job descriptions on the adjoining pages.

Job descriptions are kept on file, available for prospective volunteers to consider. The descriptions must be updated as conditions change. Job descriptions become the basis for negotiation with persons about what they are able and willing to do. Sometimes two or more persons can team up to carry out one defined task. This possibility can be an encouragement to older volunteers who hesitate to "take on too much."

3. Design Tasks to Fit the Worker

While it is helpful to have job descriptions, take care that the job descriptions are not based upon an ideal vision of the perfect volunteer. For example, a church school teacher may be expected, according to a job description, to play piano, lead singing, teach art, tell stories, and be good at crafts and games, as well as know the Bible and church history and be an authority on child psychology. It may be that this description will have to be divided up so that the "teacher"

Sample Job Description for Volunteer

Position: Driver for Meals on Wheels

Date: Tuesdays, 11:30 A.M. to 1:00 P.M. beginning March 4, 1980

Term: Continuing until further notification

Purpose: Enable older persons to stay in their own homes by deliv-
                     ering food for those unable to prepare own meals

Responsibility: Deliver meals promptly and regularly, at 12 noon

Responsible to: Volunteer coordinator of Meals on Wheels program

Responsible to Supervise: No one

Time Required: One to two hours each week on assigned day. If unable to
                     deliver on assigned day for any reason, supervisor is to be
                     notified at earliest opportunity, but not later than 9 A.M.
                     Supervisor will secure replacement.

Qualifications: Owns a car which volunteer can drive and which is ade-
                     quately insured. Desires to give assistance and supportive
                     care to older persons. Will enjoy brief visit with recipient of
                     meals.

Training: Will accompany another experienced driver to become fa-
                     miliar with procedures before beginning date. Will visit
                     Swope Ridge Health Care Center where meals are pre-
                     pared as arranged by supervisor. Will attend an occasional
                     meeting of drivers as may seem desirable, usually not more
                     than two a year.

January 15, 1980

The Shepherd's Center
Kansas City, Missouri

Sample Job Description for a Volunteer

Downtown Child Development Center

Purpose:	To provide an intensive educational experience for two- and three-year-old children who do not need full day care
Location:	Augsburg Lutheran Church, 845 West Fifth Street
Area served:	Downtown Church Center, target area above I-40
Contact:	Associate Director at the Downtown Center
Title:	Teacher aide
Description:	Volunteers to help the staff implement intensive educational and social experiences for children attending a day center. Assignments are made each day so volunteers may have different experiences.
Time:	Monday–Friday, 9 A.M. to 12 noon. Volunteers need not always stay the whole time.
Commitment:	Volunteers are asked to make a two-month commitment for a specific morning each week.
Training:	Monthly workshops, observation.

Sample Job Description for Volunteers
Service Guide for Volunteers

Name of Supervisor_____

Type of Volunteer Job_____

No. of Volunteers Needed_____

Location of Work_____

Day(s)_____

Hours   From_____To_____

Duties: (Describe the duties of the job, regular and some indication of occasional responsibilities. Explain purposes and function in relation to agency.)

Special Requirements: (Give information on specific skills, personal characteristics needed to perform in the assignment, if any. Give specifics in regard to seasonal needs, physical demands, age, sex, and limitations.)

Training: (Indicate type and length of time.)

Supervision by:_____

_____

becomes a team of persons, each of whom can bring some special competence to the total task.

Or, again, the job may have to be designed to use as much time as the person is prepared to give, such as being available on alternate Tuesdays rather than every Tuesday. There are some things that persons can do at home, from a wheelchair in a nursing home, or in a center, such as stuffing envelopes, telephoning, and knitting. One may have to take the work to them rather than have them come to the work.

As a matter of fact, however useful job descriptions are, common sense suggests that they not dominate. The job needs to be shaped within reason to fit the style, the capacity, and the concerns of the volunteer.

4. Budget Resources Needed to Support Workers

It is necessary to list tools, equipment, and resources that will be needed by the workers. This may involve transportation, a place to work, materials to work with, expense money for training, and attendance at conferences.

Decide What Has to Be Done by Paid Workers and What by Volunteers

It is important to separate the tasks which need to be paid for from those which might well be done by volunteers.

1. Factors in the Decision

a. What can the professional afford at this time? Many programs begin with volunteers but eventually evolve into an extensive organization requiring full-time professional staff and an extensive budget.

b. How much time and expertise are essential? Tasks which require considerable expertness and full-time commitment almost invariably demand that the persons who do them be paid. The person who can devote full time to a job for a dollar a year or no pay at all is exceedingly rare.

c. How satisfying and fulfilling is the work itself? Onerous, unskilled tasks usually do not appeal to volunteers. Furthermore, there is a sense in which professionals should not ask volunteers to take on any task which they would not be willing to do themselves.

d. How much participation of the membership is essential, and what roles can the members be expected to take? Another way to put this is, In what do members need to be involved for the sake of their own growth? What would they lose if they did not have an opportunity to contribute these volunteer services?

2. Professionals Evaluate Their Activities

Professionals often find this exercise useful in thinking about what they do in relation to what others can do or should be doing. Make three columns. In the first column the professional lists first what he or she did in the past week or so; below that is listed what he or she would have liked to accomplish but was not able to. In the second column he or she puts down the name of any other staff member to whom this could appropriately have been delegated and who might have done it better. In the third column the professional puts a check mark and, if possible, lists names of volunteers who might have done those tasks. (See the adjacent chart "Analysis of Activities.")

Recruit Volunteers

Whose reponsibility is it to look for and recruit volunteers? This may be approached in different ways. There seem to be three basic models of responsibility for recruitment.

1. Catch-as-Catch-Can Model

The first model may be called the Catch-as-Catch-Can Model. In this model each subunit in the organization operates independently and is responsible for finding persons to fill the volunteer slots. The problem with this model is that groups

Analysis of Activities

Instructions: First, list in the left-hand column all the things you have done during the week. Second, list those things which you would have liked to do but could not. Then go over each activity and ask yourself if it could have been done by someone else. Name in the second column a staff member to whom it could have been delegated. In the third column describe a volunteer who might be able to do it.

Tasks Done by Me	Tasks Which Could Have Been or Could Be Delegated	
	to a staff member	to a volunteer
Set up a committee meeting	secretary	
Plan the board meeting		
Write routine letters	secretary (with forms)	
Visit shut-ins		
Buy refreshments		committee member
Deliver bulletin copy to the printer		publicity committee
Plan the worship service		
Write a sermon		
Tasks I Did Not Do		
Clip magazines for the file		volunteer staff of readers
Put up a bulletin board display		

may be in competition for the same persons, and this may lead to conflict and hard feelings between groups. Also, some persons may be overlooked because the knowledge base of each group is somewhat limited. Obviously this model works best in the small church or small organization where almost everyone knows everyone else and where relationships and responsibilities are worked out informally.

2. The Pyramid Model

The second model may be called the Pyramid Model, with a few persons at the top and many at the base. In this model a key person or small group of persons selects and recruits the key co-ordinators or heads of subunits in the organization. This small group may take the form of a personnel-nominating committee that fills out the organizational chart for the heads of groups and working units. Then these coordinators in turn are responsible for recruiting the persons they need to help them in their tasks. In fact, they may, in turn, delegate to the third-level people whom they have recruited the task of filling the fourth-level jobs. The advantage of this model is that there is a large measure of involvement in the process, and the people who do the work have picked those with whom they feel comfortable in working. The disadvantage again may be that there can be competition and conflict or that the workers may not know many potential volunteers.

3. The Centralized Volunteer Service Model

The third is the Centralized Volunteer Service Model. In this model there may be a director of volunteer services who works as a staff member with a personnel committee in coordinating the process of finding, recruiting, and training volunteers. In this model the committee would be responsible for conducting a talent search, keeping a talent bank, and listing the jobs to be filled. It would coordinate the leadership training program. Obviously the committee would need to work with the coordinators of the subunits. This would not preclude having persons present themselves for service or stop persons from recruiting their friends from working with them.

Probably most organizations will have a mixture of these models.

Ways Volunteers Come to Be Involved

Volunteers are recruited in a number of ways.

1. Volunteers Present Themselves

There are volunteers who present themselves and offer to give their time. Perhaps they have been involved in the program in some way as participants. Perhaps they have friends who are already involved as volunteers. Perhaps they are seeking channels for their particular skills. They may have been active in similar programs in places where they formerly lived and want to continue the same kind of activity here. If your present volunteers are enjoying their work and are enthusiastic about it, and if it is clear that volunteers are welcomed and rewarded, other persons will volunteer. If prestige is attached to service, some may seek it out on that account. If you have a list of things that need to be done and jobs to be filled, you will be able to match their interests and abilities with the tasks.

Many persons retire with the expectation of finding interesting ways of investing their time. They either seek out volunteer service or are open to opportunities to be involved.

However, most persons will not be aggressive about presenting themselves for volunteer service. They will wait to be discovered.

2. Volunteers Respond to General Appeals

Volunteers may be recruited through general appeals, such as announcements in the church paper or in local newspapers, talent survey questionnaires, and public appeals for persons to come forward to take volunteer responsibilities. There are some problems with this broadside approach: (*a*) It usually is rather nonproductive, apart from expensive advertising; (*b*) it may call forth persons who are difficult to place and who may have to be screened out; (*c*) persons who sign up on a questionnaire and are not called on will be frustrated or will feel rejected.

There are some ways to appeal to potential volunteers so that persons who are interested and, to some degree, motivated will respond. These methods include the following.

Periodic Commitment Sundays

Many churches and organizations have a time when they distribute lists of needed services and the people are asked to indicate their interest. Follow-up, contacting those who indicate interest, is important. Do not ask people to sign up if you do not intend to respond. When persons who are not suited sign up, they can be steered to other activities. Frequently persons are reluctant to reveal their talents and interests because of modesty or for fear someone will take advantage of them.

General Mailings or Posting of Available Jobs

The commitment Sunday may be supported by displays on bulletin boards, an open file of jobs to be filled for members to examine, or information sent through the mail. This may reach some persons who are not present on particular days when volunteer service is being emphasized. It may provide a means of giving those who are interested a chance to get more information about possibilities. Displays may intrigue persons and pique their interest.

An Open House or Visitation Day

An open house planned especially for the purpose of getting persons acquainted with what is going on and what volunteers are doing may lead other persons to get interested enough to be willing to volunteer. This might be a good thing to hold immediately in advance of a commitment campaign. During such visits, job descriptions could be displayed. Descriptions of what could be done if volunteers were available and testimonies by already involved volunteers about what their work means to them may encourage persons who have not done so to volunteer or to accept an invitation to get involved.

The Every Member Talent Canvass

It is possible periodically to select and train a team of canvassers to call on persons with a view to enlisting volunteers. They should take with them a list of jobs that need to be filled and job descriptions. They should be prepared to put persons in touch with the appropriate person to discuss a particular position if interest is expressed.

Enlisting volunteers by approaching them individually is the most effective method. Such recruitment can occur naturally in the following ways.

The Membership Induction Interview

Membership organizations such as congregations have a definite advantage. They can enlist potential volunteer workers in the process of inducting new members or during the process of membership training. Some organizations using volunteers ask persons to fill out an application blank like the one shown on an adjacent page.

Vocational Counseling in Pastoral Care

Some have suggested that each person ought to take an inventory of his or her life annually. Listening to persons' reflections on what they are doing, what they are feeling, what they are learning, and how they are spending their time may yield new data which will be useful to the person and to the organization. This conference may be conducted either by the clergy or by specially trained lay volunteers.

Sample Application for Regular Individual Volunteer Service

Last Name	First	Middle Initial	Spouse's Name	Birthdate

Address		Zip Code	Home Phone	Business Phone

Present Name of School	Campus Address	Zip Code

Education–Show highest grade completed. Elementary_____ High School_____ College_____ Degrees_____

Major Subjects

Other (Business, Trade, Nursing, etc.)

Foreign Language(s)	Read	Write	Speak

Major Work Experience–Show type and length of time.

Volunteer Experience (hospital, clinic, community/church organizations)–Show type and length of time.

List major interests, hobbies, etc. Include experience and any training.

List major community or other organizations to which you belong.

Sample Application (continued)

Do you have dependable transportation?   Yes_____ No_____

Specify any health limitations.

If necessary, would you be willing to get a doctor's certificate?   Yes_____ No_____

In an emergency whom should we notify?

Name _____   Relationship _____

Address _____   Telephone _____

Availability

TIME	MON.	TUE.	WED.	THU.	FRI.	SAT.	SUN.
Morning							
Afternoon							
Evening							

Check (√) for preferred time.
Check (√√) for second choice.

How many hours can you serve regularly each week?_____

Show time of year when you will be unavailable._____

Date_____ Signed_____

(Used by permission of Volunteer Resources Department, Norristown State Hospital, Norristown, Pa.)

The leaflet "Toward Identifying Our Talents/ Gifts" by Richard Broholm is recommended for individuals reflecting alone or in a group setting. Broholm asks the readers to make a list of the things they have enjoyed doing over a period of time, from five to thirty years or even over a lifetime. Then persons are asked to star those activities valued and enjoyed the most, to describe briefly for each of these activities the talent or gift they were able to use, describe the situation or setting in which they used the talents and gifts, consider if and how they are now using these talents, and determine what this means in terms of the ministry they have the capacity to share.[2]

Older people may discover that there are things they have not done for many years, things in which they once were interested but were never able to pursue. To reactivate their talent, they may want to take a refresher course or additional training. To test their interest, they may need to have opportunities to observe the talent in use or to serve an apprenticeship.

Churches could involve their membership in the Broholm talent update process periodically by distributing the guide to each member or by organizing group settings to carry out this review.

The Preretirement Planning Interview

When one is working with older persons, it is important to be aware of their plans for impending retirement. Many of them may be in the process of considering what they will retire *to,* for the emphasis always should be on retiring *to* something rather than *from* something. This may be the opportune time to assist them in finding new activities to replace those lost when they retire.

Volunteers Who Are Already Active

A leader of a group who is alert to members'

interests and abilities may often be in a position to note talent and suggest ways the talents can be more widely used. Sometimes if prospective volunteers are asked to come in one time and do one thing, they might be intrigued enough to do it again. After they get better acquainted with the program, they might discover that they would like to spend more time participating in it.

3. Volunteers Are Recruited Personally

There are volunteers whom you recruit after you have written the job descriptions. Probably most of your volunteers will come through this source. Most of them will be members of your organization. And, in fact, if many of the members are already acting as volunteers, those who are not may expect that they will at some time be tapped. Here the church is in a unique position because induction into membership should include information about expectations with regard to the ministry of the laity and an interview about what the new members can do and would like to do. If it is not possible to involve new members immediately, this information should be on file for ready reference when positions open up for which volunteers are needed. (See chapter 6 for more details on recruitment of individuals.)

Again, a part of the process of pastoral care and Christian nurture would involve getting to know the members of the church and recording their needs, interests, abilities, and commitments. Here is affirmed that the ministry of the laity through volunteer service takes many forms and occurs through many avenues. The laity may find its ministry through the church organization, serving when the congregation is gathered for worship and study and fellowship and also when the congregation is scattered throughout the community. Individuals might be helped to see that their Christian vocation is not to serve on a church board or committee but to run for public office, accept responsibility on the board of the United Way, or work in a labor union or political party or an

[2]Richard R. Broholm, "Toward Identifying Our Talents/Gifts" in *Ministry of the Laity Packet* (Valley Forge: American Baptist National Ministries, 1979), adapted, reprinted, and distributed by permission. © 1979 The Laity Project, Andover Newton Theological School, Boston, MA.

organization devoted to a cause. Church members work in hospitals, settlement houses, youth agencies, and many other similar programs. Such programs would be impossible, in fact, without the volunteering of church members.

You need not be limited to your own members. Volunteers may be recruited from outside the organization, particularly if some special talent is needed which may not exist among your members. These persons will usually be found through personal contact and through reference by other members.

4. Volunteers Come from Volunteer Bureaus

One other source which might be drawn upon, particularly for community-wide, nonparochial, or nondenominational programs is local voluntary action centers, volunteer bureaus, or senior volunteer programs. In some cases you may want to refer members of the church to these clearinghouses of information about volunteer opportunities, especially if you have no immediate need for the services of a particular member who is eager to have something significant to do in the community.

Regardless of the way volunteers are found and recruited, many churches and communities overlook potential sources of volunteers because of negative stereotypes about age groups, such as youth or older people, about sexual roles which may preclude either men or women, about education in which it is assumed that persons with little schooling are either incompetent or cannot learn, and ethnic groups whose whole populations are excluded. Individuals may be stereotyped, as unlikely to be volunteers, on the basis of some physical characteristics, appearance, or area in which they live.

Prepare a Back-Up Group of Volunteers

Leadership training is an integral part of the total educational program of a congregation. Persons who do not feel prepared to take needed positions can gain confidence in their capacity if they have opportunities to learn. Those who have expressed interest but who have had no experience or training need to have some training, both to test their interest and to prepare for what they will be asked to do. Training opportunities may begin with self-inventories or with a general course on the ministries of the church. Specialized courses for specific ministries and jobs and also courses in theology and Bible, in listening skills, in anything that supports the volunteers and adds to their enjoyment of their work are appropriate for the church to sponsor.

Create and Keep a Talent Bank

The process of securing volunteers will be made much easier if there is a complete and reliable talent bank. This is a record system in which the experience, interests, abilities, and skills of persons are listed. To be useful, the bank has to make retrieval of the information from the system fairly easy. It is too laborious, for example, to skim through a thousand file cards to find a pianist. The process is workable if there is some kind of an index or category system.

Information to Be Recorded

No matter what form or system is used, the talent bank will have at least the following information:

Name
Address
Telephone number
Birthdate
Membership information (baptism, confirmation, etc.)
Education
Experience
A list of special interests and skills
Indication of availability

Forms of File Systems

The information as listed above may be kept on a card or a standard-sized sheet of paper. It may be kept alphabetically in a loose-leaf notebook or in a regular drawer file.

Some kind of index is needed. One kind of index is a listing of the names of those who have a particular kind of skill, interest, or experience. This index would be made up as the individual cards come in and are analyzed. Or in order to avoid the work of copying the information onto indexes, there are various ways of indexing the card or sheet itself, such as the visible index system of tabs or the system of cutting out notches so that cards in a certain category fall out when rods are inserted through the file. Many denominational stores sell systems already developed. Commercial firms will help churches plan and print up systems to meet their particular needs.

In Summary

The successful recruitment of volunteers depends in large part upon the way the stage is set. It depends upon how clear the organization is about its mission and whether or not members have been informed about their responsibility for it. It depends upon the extent to which the talents, interests, and schedules of persons are considered, as well as upon the responsibility they have to those who recruit.

The building of a strong volunteer program requires that the groundwork is carefully done. This takes time. There is no substitute.[3]

[3]See the manual on planning by Richard Lynch, *Planning for Success: A Strategy for Community Service Programs* (Washington, D.C., and Boulder, Colo.: VOLUNTEER: The National Center for Citizen Involvement).

Chapter 6

Call Volunteers into Ministry

Inspiration may come from the big dream of God's plan of salvation for all of creation and from knowing that we have a role in the dream.

But ministry begins with one person taking one step or doing one thing. What the person does in that first step depends not only upon what is needed by those who hurt but also on who the person is who is available and on what he or she can do or learn to do. The ministry of a congregation depends ultimately upon its ability to find those who will respond to a call to ministry in a specific place at a specific time to serve in specific ways among specific persons.

It is the task of those responsible for recruitment to identify likely prospects for services needed.

Conduct a Recruitment Interview

From whatever source volunteers come, an interview and a process of screening are essential. It is a mistake to assign persons to jobs for which they are not prepared or in which they cannot become competent. No volunteer should be subjected to automatic failure.

Recruitment is likely to be most successful if the prospect can be interviewed in a face-to-face conference rather than by telephone or by letter. Responsible recruitment needs to be in advance, not as a last-minute emergency.

1. Make an Appointment in Advance

The prospect should be contacted ahead of time and an appointment made for a time when the interview can be conducted free from distraction. The purpose of the conference should be specified, such as, ''I want to tell you about the work of our church, and I'd like to talk with you about the possibility of getting involved in our ministry as a member of our pastor's advisory committee during this next year.''

The interview might take place in the prospect's home or, if he or she would like, at the place where the service is to be performed.

2. Prepare for the Interview

An interview which interprets the work of a church, or unit thereof, and solicits the services of a prospect needs to be supported by any available printed material that describes the organization, its purposes, and the particular work you are asking the person to do. Try to visualize how this particular person will fit into the program. What supports and what rewards can be offered? Learn about the person's interests that match your situation. Usually a recruitment interview takes on more significance if two persons, such as co-workers or officers of the organization, accompany the recruiter. Be sure you have the written job description with you and any manuals or guides which may have been prepared for the position.

3. Present the Challenge

If the prospective volunteer is not well known to the interviewers, then the interview begins by getting acquainted, i.e., by ascertaining the interests, the background, the training, the attitudes, and the aptitudes of the prospect. Encourage the person to talk about what he or she has done and likes to do.

Ask the prospect how much he or she knows about your organization or program.

Then tell the person about the organization, about your hopes, your dreams. Tell about the human needs that the program attempts to meet. Describe specific ways the person will be serving and those with whom he or she will be working. It is important that he or she understand the purpose of the program—how progress will be measured and work evaluated.

Tell about time requirements, training opportunities, nature of staff meetings, and expenses involved. The satisfactions and the frustrations should be mentioned as well as potentialities and constraints. Do not skip over any difficulties or problems about which the volunteer should hear. Tell him or her who the supervisor will be and what help the volunteer can expect from others.

4. Give Time to Consider

It is best not to press for an immediate decision. Indicate that you want the prospect to study the material, think it over, and talk with members of the family about it. Suggest that the prospect might want to visit the program and observe it in action and talk with those with whom he or she might be working. Indicate that you will be available to answer any additional questions that might arise and that you will be in touch again.

The exception to this procedure would be when soliciting for tasks which are small or very short-term; usually such solicitation can be answered immediately with a yes or no.

5. Set a Time for Checking Back

Depending upon the situation, you may make another appointment for an interview or agree to have a telephone conversation. In some cases, if the prospect is to be out of town for a time, a letter might be the next contact. If the prospect prefers to initiate the time for giving an answer, the latest time should be agreed upon as to when the answer will be given.

6. Check Back as Often as Needed

In some cases a series of discussions might be needed before an agreement is reached, depending upon the magnitude and importance of the task you are asking the volunteer to perform. In some cases, the volunteer is interested in taking the job but has to relinquish other duties or fulfill certain obligations before being free to take it.

7. Be Open to Refusal, Delay, or Another Assignment

The volunteer who functions best and receives the most satisfaction from work is the one who freely decides to do it in light of all the factors involved. A reluctant, hesitant, or diffident acceptance is not promising. The conversation may disclose that the prospect is already engaged in a significant ministry elsewhere, is weighed down by other obligations, or prefers to become involved in your organization at another point. In any case the interview can be a supportive and clarifying experience for the prospect. It may turn out that the prospect needs ministry before he or she is free to minister to others. The prospect may be involved in the program as a participant rather than as a leader. The prospect may want to enroll in some leadership training experiences before taking on responsibility for service.

Screen Volunteers

The interview may disclose that the potential volunteer may not be as capable or appropriate as you had hoped. Or it may become clear that he or she would serve far better in other capacities. While it may be hard to reject a volunteer, it is no kindness to volunteers to involve them where they do not fit. You may suggest other types of jobs, or you may want to indicate that in light of your conversation, the position originally discussed is not the appropriate one.

Clarify and Cement the Contract

Traditionally a contract is defined as the situation which exists when an offer is made, when the offer has been accepted, and when there is an exchange of benefits. Any kind of ongoing relationship between persons partakes of the nature of a contract. The terms of the contract are the expectations which each has about the relationship, what each expects to receive and what each expects to give, how long the relationship will last and when it will end. It is important to have these expectations out in the open to be sure they mesh with one another. Otherwise there will be conflict or disappointment in the relationship over what is thought to be a breach of contract.

In order to avoid misunderstandings and conflicting expectations, it helps to have the relationship defined in writing as well as reviewed orally.

1. Go Over the Job Description Together

Give a copy of the job description to the volunteer. Read it through together. Discuss any questions raised. Check to see if the volunteer understands what is written there in the same way

you do. The process for changing or renegotiating the job description needs to be spelled out. In some cases, the job description needs to be rewritten to correspond to the agreement.

2. Send a Memo of Welcome and of Understanding

A warm and friendly letter of welcome from the head of the organization or the pastor of the congregation adds significance to the agreement of the volunteer to take on a particular responsibility. Also, it provides an opportunity for setting down in writing what is understood to be the mutual expectations, what will be expected of the volunteer, and what the volunteer may expect from fellow workers and from the organization.

3. Sign a Formal Contract

Some persons may feel that a formally signed contract is rather formal and frightening in a volunteer organization. However, a number of churches and organizations have used them with great success. Probably such contracts would be most useful only for long-term commitments and for particularly responsible positions. A form similar to the one shown on the adjacent page might be useful.

4. Hold a Commitment Service

A service of commissioning or commitment underscores the significance of the volunteer role, provides recognition of the volunteer, introduces the volunteer to the rest of the congregation, and gives opportunity to reaffirm expectations. It also stimulates the deepening of commitment and anchors it in a public affirmation.

A sample commitment service is presented here.

A General Service for the Commissioning of Volunteers in Ministry

The Call (read by the liturgist):
Brothers and sisters: We have been called to

Sample Mutual Agreement for Volunteer Service

It is hereby understood that _____ has agreed to serve as _____ in the _____ of _____ from _____ to _____ .

What Is Expected of the Volunteer

A firm commitment to the agreed-upon task.
To represent the values and ideals of the church as a faithful member.
To be on time.
To notify the supervisor as early as possible of any necessary absence.
To attend staff meetings.
To participate in at least one week of continuing education.
To be prepared to do what has been agreed needs to be done.

What the Volunteer Can Expect

The active and constant support of the supervisor.
Orientation to the task and periodic training sesssions.
Opportunity to grow through study, worship, and fellowship.
Equipment and resources to help you do your job.
Opportunities to participate in the planning of the ongoing program.
Recognition for service.

Our Mutual Contract

We hereby enter into a mutual covenant to work together in the ministry of the church for the fulfillment of our calling in Christ and the completion of God's purpose for his creation.

Signed by_____   Signed by_____
Date_____   Date_____

(This is modeled after a contract printed in Kenneth D. Blazier's *Building an Effective Church School* [Valley Forge: Judson Press, 1976], pp. 60-61.)

be disciples of Christ. We have been destined from the beginning of the world for his ministry of reconciliation. We have been redeemed and set free for fullness of life in his service. We were ordained at our baptism to seek and to save the lost, to care for the sick, to visit the friendless, to feed the hungry, to set the prisoners free, and to spread abroad the sacred and imperishable message of salvation.

We respond to the love we have experienced by committing ourselves to love God with all our being and our neighbor as ourselves. Our ministry is our song of thanksgiving to our Redeemer. Our service is our hymn of praise to our Maker.

Do you affirm your commitment to witness faithfully to God's Word and to communicate his love to others?

The Response: We do.

The Charge (read by the liturgist):

When the church, the company of disciples, gathers for worship, for study, and for fellowship, each of us has been given a responsibility. Some of us have been set apart for the ministries of the Word. Some of us have been selected to serve in the ministries of the tables.

When the church is scattered throughout the community and the world, each of us will represent the church as a minister to individuals, to families, and to organizations. We will witness to our faith in our work, our play, our friendships, and our citizenship.

The Scriptures (read by the liturgist):

Hear now these words from Paul's first letter to the Corinthians:

There are varieties of gifts, but the same Spirit; and there are varieties of service, but the same Lord; and there are varieties of working, but it is the same God who inspired

them all in every one. To each is given the manifestation of the Spirit for the common good (12:4-7). For just as the body is one and has many members, and all the members of the body, though many, are one body, so it is with Christ. For by one Spirit we were all baptized into one body . . . (12:12-13). Now you are the body of Christ and individually members of it. And God has appointed in the church first apostles, second prophets, third teachers, then workers of miracles, then healers, helpers, administrators, speakers in various kinds of tongues (12:27-28). So faith, hope, love abide, these three; but the greatest of these is love. Make love your aim, and earnestly desire the spiritual gifts . . . (13:13–14:1).

Do you acknowledge the gifts which you have received and accept the responsibility for the care and use of these gifts in Christ's name?

Response: We do.

(Here specific charges may be given to particular persons for their special responsibilities. Holy Communion may be made a part of this service. If not, go directly to the closing Prayer of Thanksgiving and of Commitment and the Benediction—the Sending Forth.)

Invitation to the Holy Communion (read by the liturgist):

If you repent of your sins and intend to live at all times lives fit for God's kingdom and to walk worthy of the gospel of Jesus Christ, draw near now in faith to participate in the sacrament of Holy Communion as he did institute and command to observe.

As the first disciples ate and drank with him on the road to Jerusalem, kept the Passover with him in the upper room on the night he was betrayed, ate supper with him in Emmaus, and knew him in the breaking of bread on the shore of Galilee after the resurrection, so we know him as we share together. Our hearts burn within us as we acknowledge his Presence among us and feel his Spirit moving with us.

Prayer of Consecration (read by the liturgist):

Almighty God, our Maker and Sustainer: Such as we are, we present ourselves for your service, aware of our limitations but trusting in your power to transform weakness into strength. When we partake of this bread, we remember how Jesus said, "This is my body broken for you. Take and eat of it." When we drink the wine, we remember how he said, "This is my blood which was shed for you. Drink of it. Do these things in remembrance."

Grant that we might be filled with his life and that we may be empowered for his ministry as members of his body and as heirs to life eternal. Amen.

(Here the elements may be distributed.)

Prayer of Thanksgiving and of Commitment (read by all or by the liturgist):

O Lord, we rejoice that you have called us into your service and that you have confirmed us in the company of those who love you. It is good for us to be on the Mount of Transfiguration for a time. Go with us now as we descend into the valley of the daily routines. Accept the service which we perform in Christ's name to his glory. Enable us to have life eternal as we participate in your creating. Amen.

The Lord's Prayer (to be said by all)

The Sending Forth (read by the liturgist):

Go forth to serve. Be prepared for your assignments. Be punctual in your appointments. Be diligent in the discharge of responsibility. Be accountable for those in your keeping. Go into all the world, proclaiming the Good News to everyone. Make disciples of all people, teaching them to observe all things commanded by God. Bring them into fellowship as brothers and sisters of one family. Do these things and our Lord and Savior, Jesus Christ, will be with you always, even unto the end of the world.

(If desired, hymns may be sung at appropriate places in the service. For example "The Church's One Foundation" might be sung between the Response to the Call and the Charge. "A Charge to Keep I Have" might be sung following the reading from the Scripture.)

Orient the Volunteer to the Task

After the agreement is reached, the volunteer must be inducted into the group or organization with which he or she is going to work, made acquainted with the setting and with co-workers, and helped to get settled comfortably in the new position.

1. Introduce the Volunteers

The volunteers may be introduced publicly to the congregation or to the assembly of the organization. Their names may be printed in newsletters and bulletins. They should be personally conducted to the place of work and introduced to co-workers. There should be an opportunity for those who are going to work together to get to know one another as persons.

2. Hold an Orientation Session for New Volunteers

All new volunteers may be brought together for a group session if they come in together or nearly at the same time. Or an orientation session for volunteers in general may be held periodically, like once every three to six months. This provides an opportunity to clarify the purposes and the philosophy of the organization. Questions can be answered. There can be general discussions about policies and programs. Responsibilities can be described. Persons may get to know those who hold other positions and see how what they do relates to other activities in the organization.

3. Provide a General Orientation Training Seminar

This is similar to the orientation session, only more thoroughgoing and involving more skill training, as well as group-building exercises. Such seminars can run from one all-day session to several days. They may take place over a series of evenings or on a weekend retreat. A suggested outline for a general orientation session is given in chapter 8.

4. Arrange a Period of Observation and Apprenticeship

Sometimes when a volunteer is to replace another volunteer, he or she can be brought in as an assistant for a time with a period of overlap between the terms of the outgoing worker and the incoming one. Or as an alternative, the new volunteer can be teamed up with an experienced worker for a time until he or she feels comfortable in taking over the responsibility. It may be that their supervisor will arrange to have the new workers observe the supervisor and work under supervision for a time to be sure that they understand what to do and how to do it.

In Summary

The calling of volunteers into ministry is an important ministry to persons. It can contribute to a person's sense of worth. It may open doors and point in new directions. It can enable persons to evaluate their activities and their values. It can be an opportunity to deepen relationships. Even though the prospective volunteer may not accept an invitation to participate, recruiting remains an aspect of pastoral ministry.

Chapter 7

Equip Volunteers for Ministry

Persons involved in the ministry of Christ not only need to be prepared for what they have been asked to do but also need to grow as they serve.

Those directing work with volunteers have an obligation to see to this. The letter to the Ephesians says,

His gifts were that some should be apostles, some prophets, some evangelists, some pastors and teachers, to equip the saints for the work of ministry, for building up the body of Christ, until we all attain to the unity of the faith and of the knowledge of the Son of God, to mature manhood, to the measure of the stature of the fulness of Christ'' (Ephesians 4:11-13).

The saints, of course, are all the members of the community of faith, each of whom is called to ministry having been made in the image of a loving, caring God. The equipment of the saints and the building up of the body of Christ to full maturity take place in a general way in the services of worship, the Bible classes, and the prayer groups. But specific growth opportunities are needed, too, through specific training for particular ministries.

Love has an obligation to be intelligent and capable. In his letter to the Philippians Paul wrote,

It is my prayer that your love may abound more and more, with knowledge and all discernment, so that you may approve what is excellent, and may be pure and blameless for the day of Christ, filled with the fruits of righteousness which come through Jesus Christ, to the glory and praise of God (Philippians 1:9-11).

Lack of preparation for and lack of continuing education in ministry can lead to failure, disillusionment, and resentment. It may also cause persons to do things which negate the purposes and intent of Christian ministry. Volunteers, no less than professionals, need training.

An understanding about competence and training is a part of the initial contract to undertake a ministry. A volunteer may already be skilled when recruited and will need very little additional training other than the initial orientation. The need for additional training may arise in the course of the program as new factors are introduced, new problems encountered, new resources become available, and new technologies of communication developed.

In addition to leadership training, the equipment of the saints calls for the provision of those material resources which are needed to carry out a program of service. Such things as space to work, materials to work with, resource books to use, and money for supplies and expenses are essential. Therefore, raising money to provide these things is another aspect of equipping the saints. In this chapter we will deal with both of these factors.

The Subject Matter of Training

Leadership training can be designed around three major categories of subject matter: what volunteers need to know, how they feel about themselves and others, and what they need to be able to do. To put it another way, they may need more information; they may need to deal with or change some of their attitudes and feelings; and they may need to develop more skill.

1. What Volunteers Need to Know

Some of the basic elements of knowledge needed by volunteers are such items as these:

The history, the mission, and the purpose of the church.

The ways in which their assignments support the basic purpose.

Facts about the assignment—the history, the people, the situational factors.

What their specific assignments are, to whom they report, for what they are responsible.

Some sense of human development.

What makes persons behave the way they do.

2. How Volunteers Need to Feel

Success and satisfaction in volunteer activity depend in part on having some of the following basic attitudes:

An acceptance of and commitment to the purpose and mission of the church.

Trust in the power of God to enable the realization of these purposes.

Confidence in their own ability to do the job.

Enjoyment in working with and relating to other persons.

Commitment to learning and growth as persons.

Awareness of their feelings about the persons and situations they will serve.

3. What Volunteers Need to Be Able to Do

Some of the basic skills needed by volunteers include

Ability to relate to and communicate with others, especially the skill of active listening.

Ability to carry out the assignments for which they are responsible.

When and Where Training Is Given

A basic tenet of education is that persons learn by what they do. Another important tenet is that persons learn most through reflection on what they are doing. Here we are talking about specific rather than general training. Opportunities for training occur in many different occasions. Some arise spontaneously. Some are planned.

1. The Recruitment Interview

Training actually begins in the recruitment interview. At this stage the volunteer is given an overview of the work of the local church or church agency as well as the working of a specific part in which he or she is being invited to participate. The materials that are left for the worker to study in the process of making a decision, such as manuals and guides and resource materials, provide needed information and instruction which is basic to the task to be performed. The job description and contract reinforce this.

2. The Orientation Process

Orientation itself is a form of leadership training. The worker is introduced to co-workers and given opportunity to exchange information and understandings about the job. The worker is shown the site of the work and introduced to the resources and equipment that will be used in the work. There will be explanations about procedures to be followed and about the policies which govern the activities. This will be an opportunity for the worker to ask questions and to reflect on and articulate feelings of discomfort, apprehension, confusion, and satisfaction experienced in this introductory period.

3. On-the-Job Training

Perhaps some of the most important learnings will take place as a volunteer encounters a problem and seeks a solution in the process of ministry. One may seek help in coping with problems and in resolving crises from a number of sources.

The Resource Library. A well-stocked and easily available library may provide volunteers with the information they need. Its availability may also be a stimulant to further study to enlarge horizons and increase effectiveness. Supervisors and counselors may direct the volunteers' attention to helpful materials by setting up displays and by putting particular resources in the hands of volunteers. A librarian should be regarded as a part of the leadership training team and a library as one of the means through which leadership training is given.

Individual Conferences. Opportunity to talk with a more experienced colleague or with one's supervisor is another way new ideas and new information are gained, skills sharpened, and vision clarified. Supervisors should set definite times for a conference with each volunteer. Opportunities for volunteers to meet together and to have time to relax with each other can be an important aspect of leadership improvement. A telephone call, a coffee break, a chat in the hallway or lounge, riding together in car pools—any of these may provide significant opportunities for learning.

Workers' Conferences. Regularly called meetings of volunteers who are working in the same area of service are useful not only for planning and evaluation but also as a means of learning and teaching. In such conferences the coordinator or supervisor can deliberately introduce new ideas, give opportunity for practice in a laboratory type situation, and clear up misconceptions. A problem becomes a prime opportunity to organize a learning session around the resolution of the problem.

4. Special Leadership Training Events

While leadership training is incidental to on-the-job reflection, research, and crisis resolution, it can become the primary focus in special training events. Such events may be preparatory, or they may be continuing education events for experienced volunteers. These may include events which use plans developed by national or regional agencies. They may be designed locally around apparent needs in specific situations.

Special Leadership Training Courses of Schools. Such carefully planned courses provide opportunity for systematic leadership training. They may be set up to involve certification of volunteers. Textbooks and training materials are available in many areas. Such courses are supplemental and complementary to the specific kinds of ministries in which persons may be engaged.

Conferences and Retreats. For many years the class meeting in a classroom for a brief period of time as a part of a course was the major form of education. In recent decades in the field of adult education the intentional, temporarily planned community has been developed as a form that is more intensive and in many ways more influential in engendering change. These events involve leaving the context of the usual routines and entering a new set of relationships in a separate environment, e.g., for a week or a weekend, where one lives with a group of persons for a time. Learning is stimulated by the intensity of the experience and also the reinforcement that comes from a community devoted to learning and to change. Camps, conference centers, resorts, motels, retreat centers, even private homes can be settings for this intensive kind of leadership training event. The focus may be on getting acquainted and team building, on deepening devotional life, on skill training, or on planning.

5. Planned Sabbatical Leaves

One of the problems encountered in any kind of work, but particularly in volunteer service, is "burnout," or fatigue. After a time the excitement and stimulation of the experience wears off, the demands of the commitment seem heavier and heavier, and interest tends to wane. Boredom and burnout may be dealt with in part by transferring the volunteer to another type of assignment with new responsibilities and a new set of relationships. In management circles this is known as "lateral promotion."

Another way of dealing with this problem is to have a policy that workers are to take sabbatical leaves after a certain period of time. But it is important that the workers are encouraged and assisted to plan for the refreshing use of their sabbatical. Sabbatical leaves may involve traveling and observing other programs. They may involve a course of reading, research, and reflection. They may include enrollment in special kinds of seminars, such as personal growth groups. They may involve a period of working on a project, such as developing a program or curriculum or writing a manual. So they include both freedom from responsibility and opportunity to have some new kinds of learning experiences.

Methods of Training Volunteers

Older adults arrive on the scene with histories of accomplishment in family, vocational, and professional life. So why consider further training for the volunteer role? Training is a support system to enable older volunteers to carry out new tasks successfully and with satisfaction to themselves. Training is to clarify and insure the standards of performance needed for the task undertaken.

Many older adults are already equipped with the skills and knowledge needed. Others may be

on new ground. Older persons' needs and desires for continuing education and psychosocial growth can be gratified through volunteer job training opportunities when these are of a quality that does justice to older persons' already acquired capacities and wisdom.

Here we enumerate some learning methods and describe them briefly, as reminders.

1. Lecture Presentation

Telling through the spoken and written word, combined with listening and hearing, is one of the oldest and most common methods. It can be most useful in making a mass of information quickly available to persons in a systematic manner. The effectiveness of this method is enhanced when illustrated with examples. Audiovisual aids help in holding attention and making points clear. Because older adults' school years occurred before some current knowledge was known, the adults' store of data on a particular subject may be archaic. A lecture can be a quick way of updating.

2. Action-Reflection

When behavioral change is the objective (such as being a better listener or responding more constructively to criticism), an action-reflection learning model is effective. The learners engage in some activity, interact with one another, or work together on a project. Then they pause to review their experience, sharing with one another what they were trying to do, how they were feeling about what was going on, and what they perceived others to be doing. Generalizations can then be drawn. Insights gained from reflection upon past experience are projected into possible anticipated experience. Practice with the new behavior provides data for further reflection.

3. Demonstration-Observation

To see a process may enable learners to grasp it much more quickly than only to hear it described. When combined with an opportunity to practice what is being demonstrated, this is one of the best ways to train persons in skills and procedures. It may take place in a laboratory situation that simulates reality, or it may take place in a real situation.

This method merges into coaching, in which a mentor works with a learner to improve performance. It frequently is extended into an apprenticeship which takes place in a real situation in which the process is observed by the student and explained by the master, who then coaches the learner as he or she practices.

4. Discussion

Opportunities to talk about what has been said and done need to accompany both lecture presentations and demonstration-observations. But even beyond that, a group may clarify ideas, develop skill in expressing ideas, and share insights in the process of talking about a situation, a problem, or a question. Leading a discussion and problem solving are skills in their own right.

5. Kickoff Case Situation

An effective way of introducing a discussion is to present a specific problem. For example, the leader might say, "You have knocked on the door of an elderly man's home for the purpose of making a friendly visit. When the door is opened and you explain that you have come as a representative of the church, he shouts that the church is full of hypocrites and he doesn't want to see you or anyone else from that church or any church. What will you do?"

Or, "You are delivering meals-on-wheels to the home of an elderly woman. No one answers the doorbell. You look through the window in the door and see her lying on the floor. What will you do and how can you get help?"

6. Case Method

The Harvard University School of Business Administration, many law schools, and schools of social work make much use of the case method of teaching. The case method requires finding a case already prepared or writing a case in which a process of problem solving has been carried through in an actual situation. The case describes decision points at which the description can be interrupted and the learners asked to make decisions, just as the real persons in the case had to do. Then the learners can test their judgment against what was actually done and what actually happened. This process is repeated a number of times as a case is carried through to a resolution.

7. Role Play

Another method which can be combined with some of the others mentioned above is role playing. In role playing the situation is described, persons take particular roles, and then they spontaneously play through the action. The role play is then analyzed and evaluated. The play may be done over again with new players or by doing the roles differently. For example, visitors might be trained by having some members of a class take the roles of persons to be visited and others the roles of the visitors. The value of this method is that persons are enabled to get inside the thoughts and feelings of those to whom they are trying to relate and so be better able to communicate with them.

8. Field Trips

Visiting other agencies and other programs can be very stimulating and illuminating. These trips will be most valuable if they are carefully prepared for and visitors go with particular things to look for or ask about in mind.

9. Seminars

Having learners do research, organize their findings, and report back is still another method of training volunteers. The seminar, which allows for discussion of what is reported, as well as participation in the development of plans for learning, usually engenders a lot of involvement and investment in the learning process.

Equipping with Material Resources

Funding is always "the bottom line" when it comes to program development. "Where can we get funds to continue to operate?" and "We need money to expand our program so that we can meet the needs we see!" are constant cries. For even if large numbers of persons give freely of their time, there are inevitable costs for office space, equipment, postage, printing, and materials. In times of inflation or recession the problem of finances becomes especially acute.

Where can churches find the funds to support additional ministries? It is estimated that in 1978 Americans gave $39.6 billion to charity. Of this amount 83 percent came from individual donors; 6.6 percent came from bequests. If we add these two figures, we see that 89.6 percent—almost 90 percent—came from individuals either directly or through bequests. Foundations gave 5.5 percent and corporations gave 4.9 percent. Obviously most of the money to support voluntary programs depends upon giving from individual donors who believe in the programs and who want to share what they have with others in this way.

However, at times those seeking support for a specialized ministry with the aging can obtain support from foundations or public agencies. An especially helpful book is *Funding Sources in Aging: Public, Private, and Voluntary,* compiled and edited by Lily Cohen and Marie Oppedisano-Reich (Garden City, N.Y.: Adelphi University Press, 1979); it is 308 pages in length and costs $14.50. Very often the funding source has a procedure it requests of applicants and a form to use. For help in preparing a proposal, see "Guidelines for Proposal Writing," Appendix B of this book.

In Summary

Since for many older people volunteer service is their career, it is important to insure that they will find satisfaction in it. Enjoyment of volunteer service depends in part upon the kind of support they receive in terms of training and material resources with which to work. Personal growth is more likely to occur when learning is planned.

Chapter 8

A Kit of Leadership Training Sessions

To be most effective, leadership training has to be designed to fit the particular situation and the particular needs of the volunteers who are to perform a ministry in that situation.

The session plans included here are suggestive and illustrative. An orientation session is included because that is useful in almost every situation. The other sessions are focused on human relations skills since almost all volunteers will be working with and relating to other persons. (See *A Handbook of Structured Experiences for Human Relations Training,* seven volumes, by J. William Pfeiffer and John E. Jones [San Diego, Calif.: University Associates, 1972], for a full discussion of human relations skills.)

A SAMPLE GENERAL ORIENTATION SESSION

Objectives

To provide information about the history, the mission, and the purpose of the organization.

To insure clarity about the organizational structure and the way decisions are made.

To describe the role of the staff in relation to the volunteers.

To inform volunteers about their rights and responsibilities.

To give opportunity for asking questions, clearing up confusion, resolving doubts.

To begin the building of a team concept and spirit.

Size of Group

Any number

Setting

The meeting should be held in or near the office or place of work so that volunteers will become familiar with the surroundings. The meeting rooms will need to be comfortable and provided with chalkboards or newsprint easels. A meeting room for all to gather, with other rooms for small group meetings, is necessary.

Provide for any audiovisual aids to be used in the presentation.

A. *GETTING STARTED* (40 min.)

1. *A get-acquainted period* (20 min.)

Have volunteers make large, easily readable name tags. Have each one create on the tag first a symbol telling what he or she is going to be doing as a volunteer and then another symbol illustrating a particular gift or talent he or she is bringing which can be used in the program.

Have them find one other person, introduce themselves, and discuss the meanings of the symbols on their name tags.

Have the pair find another pair. Let them share previous experiences in volunteering or experiences which can be drawn on for use in what they are going to be doing.

2. *Identify procedures of the meeting* (5 min.)

Leader and participants list and discuss these elements:

 a. A period of presentations and discussion
 b. Volunteers and supervisors/coordinators meeting in small groups for specific orientation
 c. Evaluation of session for fulfillment of expectations
 d. Closing worship

3. *Clarify purposes and expectations for this meeting* (15 min.)

Leader states hoped-for outcome (where the group will be at the end of this meeting) and lists it on newsprint.

In small groups have participants identify where *they* hope they will be; report these hopes to leader and total group and then list them on newsprint.

Compare lists. Deal with discrepancies.

B. *PRESENTATION/DISCUSSION PERIOD* (45 min.)

1. *Input of facts/figures/history of project* (15 min.)

Participants in pairs discuss how this is what they expected; opportunity to question speaker for further clarification.

2. *Identify what is implicit in this project that reflects the mission and purpose of the sponsoring organization (church)* (20 min.)

Preferably let the participants in small clusters make this identification and report their ''findings.'' Leader can endorse, correct, and amplify as appropriate.

3. *Leader describes essentials of the sponsoring*

organization that bear on this volunteer project: how policies are made, how programs are evolved and funded, personnel and staff specifically dealing with this project. (10 min.)

Invite questions for clarification.

C. *SMALL GROUPS/SUPERVISOR SESSION* (30 min.)

Each group moves to another room or corner with a supervisor to discuss specifics of its assignment.

D. *EVALUATION SESSION* (15 min.)

In small clusters in plenary session, participants identify what they feel good about as a result of today and where they want more support. An alternative method, if time is short, is to hand out cards for each person to write his or her own answers to what was good and what else is wanted. (This is important material for follow-up.)

E. *CLOSING PRAYERS* (10 min.)

A SAMPLE LEADERSHIP TRAINING SESSION
TRAINING IN COMMUNICATION SKILLS: LISTENING ACCURATELY

Objectives

To sharpen participants' appreciation of the importance and the difficulty of communication and especially of the importance of hearing accurately not only the words but also the meanings of what others say or tell.

To impress upon the participants that to insure accuracy of perception, it is important to check one's understanding with the communicator. (Understanding the meaning is more than merely hearing the words.)

To increase skill and begin the formation of a habit of checking one's hearing, which constitutes hearing both words and meaning.

Size of Group

Maximum of 24, minimum of 8.

Setting

A comfortable meeting room, reasonably

free of distractions and interruptions, with persons seated in a circle or a horseshoe formation.

Chalkboards or newsprint easels should be available, on which main points of learning can be recorded, illustrating another principle that multimedia communication usually is more effective than "monomedia" communication.

Approach

Invite participants to identify main communication problems they have experienced in their situations. List these problems, offering your own experience and the data that you gathered from your preparation for this session.

Rather than talking more about communication, move on to an exercise which enables the participants to note directly how their experiences in this session are like the insights they and you reported above.

Use the old parlor game of Gossip. Whisper a message into the ear of the person next to you, and ask him or her to pass it on to the next person and so on until the message has gone around the circle. The last person to receive the message tells what he or she has heard. Is the message as given originally? How has it changed? Where did the shift take place?

A variation on this is to send several persons out of the room. Then call one of them back. You or someone in the group relates to that person a story with some details in it. For example, "As I was coming to this meeting, I heard sirens blowing; and when I got to the intersection of Broad and Main, I saw that a fire truck had almost collided with a school bus, but in order not to hit the children, it had plowed into the front of a grocery store. Several firemen were badly injured. People were standing around. There were vegetables all over the street. The ambulance arrived just as I came by." The listening person now is to convey the story to the next person, who is called in from the outside. Have each succeeding person tell it to the next until all who were sent out of the room have been called back in and have

heard the story. At that point the original story is repeated so all can see how it has varied in the telling. Obviously the audience will have noted the continuing distortions in the storytelling. The more exciting the story, the more likely the distortions. Ask the persons who listened and retold the story to recall what was going on inside them, where their attention was focused, and what they were feeling.

Procedure

Tell the group that it is possible to focus on the communication or on the receiver of the message. Usually we focus on the communicator and try to think of ways he or she can speak to convey a message more accurately. However, the receiver is as important to the process as the sender of a message, and in this session we are going to focus upon the hearer, or receiver.

Ask, "What could have been done by the hearer to insure that he or she perceived more accurately?" Discuss. Receive suggestions and list on the chalkboard or newsprint.

Say that one of the most effective ways of insuring that a message has been heard accurately and understood is to repeat it to the communicator and ask if the repetition is what the communicator said or intended to say. Give a demonstration of what you mean by having a member of the group share an opinion about an event or activity in the community. Then check your understanding of his or her statement by repeating it to the person.

At this point tell all the group members that for the next twenty minutes they are to carry on a discussion, but that no one can express his or her own ideas until he or she has repeated accurately to the speaker's satisfaction the meaning or opinion the previous speaker expressed.

A variation which is good to use in a large group, as it gives more persons opportunity to participate, is to divide the participants into groups of three. Give them a topic to discuss that will enable them to communicate an opinion. One member of each group is to express the opinion.

The second member, who is the listener, is to feed it back to the communicator to see if he or she has been understood. The third member is to observe the process. After a few minutes call time and have the observer become the communicator, the listener become the observer, and the first communicator become the listener. Do this until each person has had opportunity to practice checking communication. In the plenary session give participants a chance to identify their learnings, especially what they learned about themselves as listeners.[1]

Close

Stress again the importance of checking our perceptions of that which we are hearing with the communicator. Give illustrations of situations in which it is most useful.

SAMPLE SESSION OUTLINE
INTERPRETING BODY LANGUAGE AND NONVERBAL COMMUNICATION

Objectives

To become aware of what is communicated through the posture and movement of the body.

To learn how to respond sensitively to nonverbal signals during the communication process.

Size of Group

Maximum of 20, minimum of 8.

Setting

For this session a discussion setting is needed, with persons sitting in a circle so that they can see one another. It is better if there is no table in the circle.

Approach

Begin with an opening statement:

Every image that comes to our minds, every idea we hold, is accompanied by a feeling. We tend to react to these images, ideas, and feelings. This reaction is expressed not only through speech but also in the way we stand, sit, walk, or move. It is expressed through the timbre of our voice.

Children tend to express themselves openly with their whole bodies. Most adults learn or are taught to hide their feelings.

Some people try to cultivate a "poker face" to mask their feelings and to try to control their bodies so that no signals are given. Even then, they may sometimes be betrayed by the movement of their feet or their hands.

Gestures, postures, and movements are a part of the message that is communicated. We often respond unconsciously to the total message even when we concentrate on the verbal message and ignore the nonverbal. Communication is improved if we learn to attend to the total message or to the sometimes contradictory messages when the verbal message is not congruent with the nonverbal message. Relationships are deeper and more genuine when we become sensitive to nonverbal messages.

Procedure

Have persons name the nonverbal messages they are aware of and to which they respond. List these on the chalkboard or newsprint. Probably they will name such things as a limp handshake, fidgeting, and sitting on the sidelines. The list could include things such as sitting apart from the group, never speaking in a group, slumping dejectedly, sitting on the back of one's spine, leaning forward toward the speaker, pounding on the table, and getting red in the face. Discuss what these nonverbal messages generally might mean.

Give each member of the group a slip of paper designating an emotion or attitude, like anger, delight, disappointment, boredom, cooperative interest, suspicion, indecision, and agreement. Each person is given opportunity to express the feeling or attitude nonverbally. Let the others try to interpret the person's actions to see if they

[1]See *Human Listening: Processes and Behavior,* by Carl H. Weaver (Indianapolis, Ind.: The Bobbs-Merrill Co., 1972), for an excellent review and fuller discussion of the art of listening. There are many training exercises on listening and community in the human relations training literature. A recent emphasis is on *active listening,* which recognizes the need to hear meanings and to respond supportively without getting involved in the speaker's agenda.

can read the physical signals and if the person can consciously communicate what he or she intends by his or her actions.

Set up a role-playing situation reflective of a typical setting in which the volunteers you are training are working. Give some of the participants private instructions about certain feelings and attitudes they are to pretend to have and to express nonverbally. Appoint several persons as observers to see if they can spot which feelings the persons are communicating.

Choose a discussion topic that can evoke both participation and a variety of positions and feelings, something controversial. Have some members of the group be observers watching for nonverbal messages. Let the discussion go on long enough to elicit enough responses to provide material for discussion.

Be sure to tell the group that just as one needs to check the accuracy of what one hears from verbal communication, one also needs to check the accuracy of what one observes in terms of nonverbal communication. Such comments as the following might be helpful: "I notice you are sitting outside the circle and seem uninterested in the discussion (or preoccupied). Am I right? Would you like to talk about how you feel?"

Bring together a number of kickoff case situations to evoke discussion. For example: Two children enter a classroom. One comes in directly without hesitation, comes to the table to fill out a name tag, and goes immediately to the library corner to select a book to read while waiting for the class to begin. The other comes in hesitantly and slowly, stands uncertainly just inside the door, looking all around. When invited to come and get a name tag, the child reluctantly picks up a tag and perfunctorily writes the name, then stands apart. How would you interpret the behavior of each child? How would you respond?

Close

Close the session with a review of the points made during the session.

SAMPLE SESSION OUTLINE
INCREASING CAPACITY FOR EMPATHY

Objectives

To make conscious the process through which we come to sense how others feel and what they must be thinking.

To increase the capacity of persons to empathize with others.

Size of Group

Maximum of 15 to 20, minimum of 10.

Setting

A room where persons can be seated comfortably in a circle.

Approach

Introduce the group to the concept of empathy. It means "to feel with." It can be contrasted with "sympathy," which means "to feel for." To empathize is to understand rather than to get caught up in the feelings and situation of the other person. To empathize allows one to make a considered and thoughtful response. To sympathize means to be carried away and along with the other or to be enmeshed in the other's problems. Empathy allows one to be helpful to the other and to assist the other to gain some perspective on the situation. Sympathy tends to consolidate the problem and increase it.

Share the objectives of the session.

Procedure

Divide the group into two subgroups. Place one group in a circle and have the other group form a circle around the inner circle. Pair members of the outer circle with members of the inner circle. The persons in the outer circle are to observe and to empathize with their partners.

Give the group in the inner circle any kind of structured exercise you wish. For example, you might have them work together to design a model home, describing what it would contain, how it should look, how large it should be, etc. (Materials such as paper and pencils should be available but not offered until requested.) Or you might give them some materials to work with, such as paper, glue, Scotch tape, pins, wooden dowels, tinker toys, etc., and instruct them to design a piece of sculpture which would express the nature and purpose of your church.

After ten minutes or so, stop the exercise and let the pair members talk to each other. The observer will share his or her perception of how the participant was feeling and what he or she was trying to do in order to check the accuracy of the observation and its interpretation.

Then the outer group takes the place of the inner group and vice versa. Another exercise is introduced and the process is repeated.

Close

Review what may have been brought out in the session. Let persons share what they have learned or have had confirmed. The point of the exercise is to remind persons to be attentive to the whole person with whom they are communicating, to listen to the tone of voice as well as the content of the words, to note the posture and movement of the body, the gestures, and the way one positions himself or herself in relation to others so as to be able to respond to the reality of the interpersonal situation.

SAMPLE SESSION OUTLINE
TAKING APPROPRIATE GROUP MEMBER ROLES

Objectives

To enable persons to become aware of the roles they usually take in group settings and to evaluate them from the standpoint of their appropriateness and helpfulness.

To become aware of the range of roles needed for a group to function most effectively.

To increase persons' skill in taking the roles needed by the group in order to perform its function.

Size of Group

A group of any size beyond a minimum of five persons, provided the group may be subdivided into groups of no more than ten to fifteen persons each.

Setting

A room where persons can sit in groups in a circle, around tables, or in chairs with arms, so they can write comfortably.

Materials Needed

Pencils and copies of the Role Designation Form (shown on the adjacent page).

Approach

Introduce the group to the concept of a role as a characteristic set of actions or a way of behaving taken in relation to other persons. Remind them that for a group to operate effectively, a number of roles are essential. Some roles relate to the task the group is trying to accomplish, some to the development and maintenance of the group. Other roles block the group and interfere with its performance. The roles that help the group may be taken by any member when that member sees they are needed. The most effective group is one in which each member does what he or she can to assist the group and in which members avoid blocking roles. Persons who customarily take negative group roles may learn to change in favor of positive roles. Persons who take only one role may learn to take others if they see that they can be helpful.

Procedure

Distribute the Role Designation Forms. See that everyone has a pencil. Look at the list of roles and insure that they are understood. Some roles have been defined here. The ''Initiator/contributor'' makes suggestions and offers ideas. The ''Information seeker'' asks questions to elicit more data. The ''Information giver'' provides data, often in answer to questions. The ''Coordinator'' tries to show how ideas and suggestions fit together or can be unified and how a problem can be attacked systematically. The ''Orienter'' helps the group to see what its situation is and where it is in the process of task performance.

Role Designation Form

Directions: Enter names of members in the spaces at the heads of the columns. For each member place a check mark opposite the role he or she has taken most often.

Roles   **Members**

Roles	A	B	C	D	E	F	G	H	I	J	K	L
Group Tasks Roles												
1. Initiator/contributor												
2. Information seeker												
3. Information giver												
4. Coordinator												
5. Orienter												
6. Evaluator												
Group Maintenance-Oriented Roles												
7. Encourager												
8. Harmonizer												
9. Gatekeeper and expediter												
10. Standard setter or ego ideal												
11. Follower												
Negative or Individually Oriented Roles												
12. Blocker												
13. Recognition seeker												
14. Dominator												
15. Avoider												

(Based on the research of Kenneth D. Benne and Paul Sheats, ''Functional Roles of Group Members,'' *The Journal of Social Issues*, vol. 4, no. 2 [Spring, 1948], pages 41-49.)

The "Evaluator" seeks to test ideas and proposals against some kind of standard. "The Gatekeeper" helps other members get into the discussion or get their ideas heard. "The Follower" supports the group actively by expressing concurrence or agreement rather than by going along passively as dead weight. The "Blocker" is against almost anything that comes up and heads off efforts to reach a decision by distracting comments and behavior. The "Avoider" leads the group off on sidetracks, etc.

If the group members have worked together before, they may be able to fill out the role Designation Forms immediately. Then they can share what they have put down and talk about the meaning of the roles the members take.

If the group is made up of persons new to one another, give them a task to perform in which they must reach decisions by consensus. For example: Develop a list of the ten most important qualities of a leader and put them in rank order with the most important on top. Then have the group use the Role Designation Form, checking the roles members have taken.

Give the group another task. This time assign some members of the group to take some of the roles, especially roles which seem to have been missing before.

As a variation of this, brief the members of the group privately or give them slips of paper designating the roles they are to take in the session. After the group has worked at its task for a time, stop to fill out the sheets and see if the members have been able to detect the roles others were assigned to take. Repeat this as often as useful and as time allows.

Close

Have the members of the group evaluate the extent to which the objectives of the session may have been achieved. Encourage them to keep working at broadening their repertoire of roles and at increasing their capacity to analyze a process to see which roles are needed at particular times. Perhaps they will want to look at the way they have worked together in the past and to identify roles that need to be supplied for the group to be more effective.

Chapter 9

Supervision—To Build Up the Body of Christ for Mission

In his letter to the Romans Paul underlined his central concept of the church as the Body of Christ: "For as in one body we have many members, and all the members do not have the same function, so we, though many, are one body in Christ, and individually members one of another" (Romans 12:4-5).

This notion of a body or an articulated system of parts working together applies to a single congregation, to a denomination, to all the denominations together, to the worldwide universal church. Whether applied to the church on a universal level or a congregation on the local level, the term "body" points to the unity as well as an organic system composed of essential parts which work together.

A body or a community needs to be built up through nurture and exercise. It needs maintenance so that when depleted, it can be restored; when wounded, it can be healed; and when challenged, it can be energized. Community building is a responsibility, a gift, and a skill in its own right, a function that needs to be attended to deliberately. In the secular sphere this is sometimes known as organizational development.

Organizational development—community building—is the process of enabling a group of persons to cope with challenges, to adapt to change, to plan for the future, and to accomplish its mission. Such development takes place by clarifying and evaluating beliefs, attitudes, and values; by reorganizing its structure; by acquiring and sharpening skills, particularly the skills of working together; by changing relationships; and by creating ceremonies to celebrate what it has received as grace from God, what it has achieved, and what it purposes to do.

Community building occurs through the behavior exemplified by its central members, through the processes of supervision, and through worship and celebration.

An organization or group takes its tone from the person or persons who sit at the center of the communication network and who serve as the central coordinators. (See in chapter 3 the section "The Professional's Relation to the Volunteer.") The way these persons relate to other persons, the way they go about coping with problems, the way they think and how they feel—all tend to be reflected by those who work with them. In the helping professions this is sometimes referred to as ''the parallel process.'' It refers to the fact that a child tends to treat other children and especially younger children as the parents treat him or her, that a client deals with others as the therapist deals with him or her, that students acquire the manner and style of their teacher.

Community building occurs in the process of supervision. It occurs in times of celebration. It occurs in the way we deal with the weakest member or the ineffective volunteer. It is supported by adequate records which enable the community to know what its members do.

Supervision Defined

Too many persons erroneously assume that supervision means checking up on and evaluating job performance, of putting pressure on workers to wring greater effort out of them in the interest of productivity for the sake of profit. Too often it inaccurately has overtones of bossiness, acrimonious criticism, demeaning of persons, and control of others. It has to be admitted that overseers sometimes do these things.

However, when true to its function, supervision is working with the volunteer to enable him or her to do the work more effectively and to enjoy the satisfaction of succeeding at the tasks he or she is trying to accomplish. In other words, supervision is a kind of partnership in which skilled and experienced workers back up a frontline worker as needed. Because some persons have negative connotations of ''supervision,'' terms like ''coordinator'' or ''counseling teacher'' are sometimes used. Whatever it is called, it is an essential function in an organization.

Who Is the Supervisor?

The supervisor is the professional or the person, paid or unpaid, in an organization who is responsible ultimately for the administrative processes. These processes include planning, staffing, directing (which includes coordinating and communicating), and control (which includes evaluation to assure that the end results are in line with objectives and purposes). In this instance the supervisor is the person on whose desk the buck stops and who is responsible for enabling others to get the work done.

Since no one person can single-handedly carry out all of these processes over the span of a large organization, this supervisory function has to be shared with others. As an organization grows larger and more complex, it has to be subdivided into units which are manageable. It is very difficult to supervise more than six or seven persons in a line relationship.

So second, or lower level, supervisors may be volunteers working with other volunteers who themselves may experience supervision. They may be heads of committees, superintendents of departments, lead teachers of teaching teams, or coordinators of task forces. In fact, co-workers may supervise one another.

In some cases the supervisor is freed from most of the other management functions so as to concentrate on this troubleshooting, enabling, suporting function. This is the concept behind the designation of counseling teachers in the educational system and of the staff consultant who functions apart form the line or chain of command responsibility.

Supervision, then, can function through two models of organization, as given below:

Supervision as a Line Responsibility

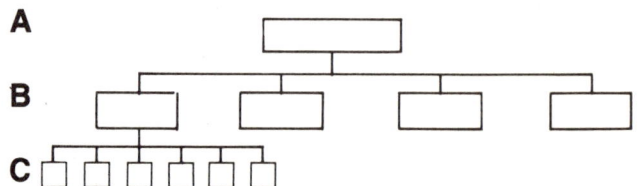

In this model the person on level A supervises the persons on level B, and they in turn supervise those on level C, who report to them.

Supervision as a Staff Function

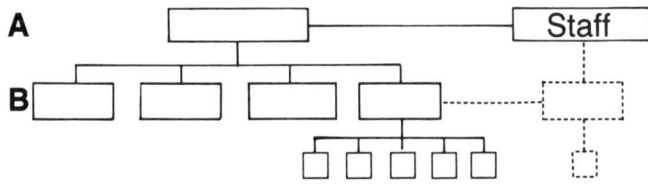

In this model those in charge on levels A and B still have supervisory responsibilities, but in addition they can call on a staff person to assist them with problem solving.

A staff supervisor, as opposed to a line supervisor, functions primarily as a consultant.

Supervision as a Consultant Process

Whether supervision is done by the persons who carry line responsibilities or by the person who is a staff assistant, when being carried out, it is a process of consultation. This means that the worker is supported, strengthened, and equipped with essential resources but that the control over and decision making about the work are left in the hands of the worker. The consultant has several functions.

1. To Help the Worker Obtain and Look at All the Relevant Facts

When problems arise, it is too easy to make snap judgments about the situation without having the information that would lead to better understanding. The consultant may possess information or may have the skill of gathering information and of checking to be sure all the facts are known. For example, the leader of a youth group may assume that a particular boy's inattention is due to disinterest and hostility. Closer observation may disclose that the boy has a hearing problem of which he may not be aware or which he is trying to cover up.

The first step in the consultation process may be to have the worker try to describe the situation as he or she sees it. This may lead to further study of the situation to get a clearer picture.

2. To Enable the Worker to Make an Accurate Diagnosis of the Problem

It is a temptation to look for simple solutions or single answers to complex situations. For example, it may be assumed that so-called juvenile delinquency results from a lack of a recreational program and play space in a community, when poverty, unemployment, social patterns, and discrimination may all be involved.

3. To Assist the Worker to Generate Alternative Solutions

The more ideas one can generate for the solution of problems, the more likely it is that a truly creative idea will emerge. Workers often get caught up in pat answers and routine responses to situations.

4. To Support the Worker in Carrying Out Own Decisions

Support is both psychological and material. In order to do what a worker decides to do about a problem, additional training or resources may be needed. Or perhaps all that is needed is encouragement.

The Supervisory Relationship

Supervision, as a relationship in which one person supports and enables others in doing their jobs so that the outcomes of their activities are congruent with the purposes of the sponsoring community, takes place in several ways.

1. A Co-worker with the Volunteer

As a co-worker, the supervisor may sit down with the volunteer and participate in planning a program, an activity, a session, or an event. In this process he or she may share information about resources, contribute ideas, raise questions, or even teach a skill. The supervisor may work alongside the volunteer in the delivery of a service, sharing the load, or taking the lead, and demonstrating what and how it is to be done. As a partner and co-worker, the supervisor does not take the responsibility out of the hands of the volunteer unless he or she relinquishes it temporarily to be shown how to act.

2. A Mirror for the Volunteer to Observe Himself or Herself

A supervisor may observe the volunteer in action in order to provide the worker with objective data about how he or she is functioning. The supervisor becomes a kind of mirror enabling the worker to get a true picture of how he or she functions or is improving function. Process notes, tape recordings, or video recordings may assist this process.

As an observer, the supervisor may also be able to gather data about the responses of those with whom the volunteer is working, which the worker may be too busy to notice in the performance of his or her duties.

3. Enable the Volunteer to Reflect on Experience

Often it is useful for volunteers to have an opportunity to sit down and reflect on their work and the situations and their relations to their co-workers. Sometimes this is spoken of as a debriefing following a session or an event of any kind. It may be done in the context of an annual evaluation of the experience. It may be called for when a problem arises that needs to be worked out.

In the process of reflection it is important to report or recall as much as possible of the experience, what happened, what feelings arose, what was said and done. Then the question can be raised of what alternatives were considered and why the particular one was chosen. What might have happened if a different alternative had been selected? Then on the basis of what is now known, what other things might have been done which

were not thought of? Finally, if a similar situation comes up again, what might be done next time?

By considering such questions, the worker is enabled to learn from the experience and to get ready for dealing with similar situations which might arise in the future.

Celebrate the Ministry of Volunteers

Celebration is as important as supervision in building up and strengthening the body of Christ. Celebration is akin to reflection inasmuch as it begins with recollections of the past and the representation of the past to the community and to consciousness. But while the process of reflection in supervision focuses upon what can be learned and what is meaningful about experience, in celebration the focus is upon thanksgiving, upon expression of appreciation, upon the highlighting of achievements and the passing of milestones, and upon the affirmation of the worth both of the project and of those who are engaged in it.

Celebration is a way to meet the needs of persons for recognition of their services to the community and for the community to express appreciation for those services. In a way a celebration is a means for people to reward themselves for being who they are and for what they have done or tried to do. It can run the gamut from the informal moment to the highly formal ceremony.

1. Provide a Moment of Recognition and Appreciation

In a well-functioning community persons get frequent strokes of approval and encouragement. A co-worker or supervisor may simply say, "I thought you did that very well. How did you feel about it?" This may give the volunteer the opportunity to say, "Thank you. I wasn't sure how it went." Or, "Thank you. I felt good about it too." A pat on the shoulder or a handshake reinforces the recognition. With most older people, especially, touch is appreciated.

In group settings it is important to say every

once in a while, "I believe we ought to note what John did and tell him how much that meant to the success of our project." Applause or verbal expressions may underscore such recognition.

2. Note the Passing of Milestones

Anniversaries, birthdays, and annual meetings provide occasions for remembering a period of time gone by and catching up its highlights in celebration. It is tempting to dwell upon failures. It is better to give thanks for gifts possessed and work well done. The anniversaries and birthdays of individuals as well as of organizations and groups can be remembered and celebrated so as to confirm the value and worth of the persons so recognized.

3. Gather for Worship and Devotion

Services or moments of worship or devotion may do two things. They may provide opportunity to focus on the concerns and celebrate the successes of individual persons. Also, they may be occasions for focusing on the concerns and achievements of the group.

4. Provide for Special Recognition Ceremonies

In addition to the kinds of recognition, expressions of appreciation and celebration that come naturally in the process of living and working together, it is desirable to plan separate and special times when the work and achievements of volunteers are honored. These may include recognition luncheons or dinners at which volunteers are the guests of honor, special awards are given for outstanding achievement or length of service, and the attention of the community is called to the importance of their contribution. Ceremonies may be held at the completion of a term of office.

Sometimes pins or certificates for a certain amount of service are given. At the very least, persons' names are called, they stand up to be seen, and they receive applause.

In addition to recognition, these programs will be most successful if they reward the volunteers with a worthwhile program, whether it be an informative and inspiring speaker, a dramatic production, or musical entertainment. A party for volunteers may meet a need and be a reward in some situations.

5. Observe National Volunteer Week

The National Center for Citizens Involvement plans and provides materials for Volunteer Week to be celebrated every May. To support the observance, it prepares a Volunteers Recognition Kit, which may be ordered from P.O. Box 1807, Boulder, CO 80306. Local voluntary action centers may sponsor community-wide observances. Local churches and agencies may capitalize on this by planning their own events to coincide.

6. Memorial Services

Memorial services held to commemorate the lives of persons who have faithfully served their communities become another important time to recall and celebrate what they have done as family members, as members of organizations, as citizens of the community. This is a way of expressing gratitude and at the same time lifting up role models for others to emulate.

Many churches observe All Saints Day or Memorial Sunday as a time to remember and to honor all the dead whose efforts have made community possible and whose lives have left their mark on others they have served. This is a time when those still living can rededicate themselves to causes and concerns which have been supported by the deceased in the past.

Cope with the Ineffective Volunteer

The dark side of working with volunteers, opposite to the struggle to find and recruit them, is the necessity which sometimes arises of terminating them for just cause when the volunteer refuses to bow out and go off the stage. Sometimes positions or titles are so important to the ego of volunteers that, in spite of inability to produce, lack of response from others, irresponsibility in performance, or antagonism to the philosophy and policies of the organization, they continue to cling to positions. So sooner or later managers of volunteers may ask: ''How can I help ineffective volunteers find other avenues of ministry? Or, if that fails, how can I dismiss undesirable volunteer workers?''

1. Clarify the Mission of the Organization

To begin with, it is essential to be clear about the mission of the organization and to have standards of performance that are widely known and against which work can be evaluated. By the same token, it is helpful to have what is equivalent to work rules, the violation of which will lead to termination. These all should be discussed in the recruitment, training, and orientation process so that volunteers understand the conditions under which they are free to quit or under which the organization is free to replace them.

2. Clarify the Vocation of the Volunteer

Second, care in selection can reduce the number of workers who are unable to perform or who are put into positions for which they are unfitted or in which they will become problems. Apprenticeships and trial periods enable the agency to evaluate the capability of the volunteer and to anticipate and head off some potential problems. The trouble usually comes when an agency is desperate for help and impulsively takes all who will say yes and puts them to work without orientation or training.

3. Make a Definite Contract

Third, it is helpful to have the length of the period of service stated in the contract from the beginning so that it is understood that at the end of the stated time there is no obligation on the part of either party to renew the relationship. This goes along with a general policy of rotation in positions. If volunteers are encouraged to take on and train apprentice replacements, this will support the idea of rotation. Some organizations also provide for sabbaticals for volunteers—every so often they are given special opportunity for training or different kinds of experiences.

4. Surround with Supports to Improve Performance

Fourth, when volunteers are falling down on the job, if adequate supervision is available, problems may be reviewed and overcome in conference between workers and supervisor. Some failures that indicate a possible need for termination may be overcome by counseling. A part of the counseling process is to enable each volunteer to understand limitations as well as strengths and to find a place to function successfully.

5. Promote Workers Laterally

Fifth, closely allied to counseling and supervision is the possibility of moving a worker to another job which is commensurate with time schedules, interests, and abilities, but which also is significant. Lateral promotion is often used in industry to overcome boredom on the executive levels by presenting new opportunities.

6. Retire with Honor

Sixth, older workers may be elevated to an honorary or emeritus status, given recognition for past services, and enabled to share their experience with the organization while retaining ties with it. Ordinarily such status is reserved for those who have served long, faithfully, and well, but who because of declining abilities or decreasing interest can no longer put as much time, energy, and capability into the position as they once did.

7. Accept Declining Capacity Constructively

Seventh, sometimes it is possible to let persons "die on the vine," and work around them when they adamantly insist on keeping on and when no harm is being done. One of the pathetic aspects of working with the elderly is that they sometimes slowly or even rapidly decline in physical and mental ability without recognizing or being able to admit that their capacities have changed. For example, a retired teacher found tremendous joy and significance in teaching a class in an adult education program in the area of her training and experience. For a number of years she was popular and respected. Then she began to fail. She had lapses of memory which became embarrassing to the members of the class. Her health failed, and she frequently was unable to meet the class, requiring the director to find a replacement at the last minute. When asked if she would consider dropping the class, she refused, insisting she would be all right, even though registrations were falling and dropouts were increasing. The solution was to find a person who understood the situation and was willing to step in as an understudy upon short notice. In the meantime she was allowed to teach her class in spite of dwindling attendance. Other classes were available in the program. So, apart from any possible negative image given to the educational program as a whole, the ego of a frail and declining woman was kept intact for a time.

8. Educate Volunteers to Cope with Aging

In working with older volunteers, one would do well to include in the training programs available to them some discussions on coping with the process of aging and possible declining strength. Persons need some help in recognizing limitations, particularly those which come invidiously, so as to deal with them gracefully and creatively. Support of the ego by loving and caring acceptance during this process enables persons to make the adjustments with much more grace. Teaching alternate ways of meeting needs for self-expression increases flexibility.

9. Terminate with Love

Finally, there may be situations in which the volunteer must be terminated—firmly, gently, courteously—for the greater good of the greater number. When a person persistently fails to comply with policies and rules of the organization which are generally known and publicly acknowledged, when a person sabotages the philosophy and mission of the organization knowingly, when a person is irresponsible or unreliable in the performance of duties or simply is unable to continue in an agreed-upon task, it may be time for termination. This comes best after counseling and conferences about the work have been tried and found unsuccessful. Termination needs to be supported by concrete and specific documentation of the reasons for termination. It is easiest when made clear that the termination is based upon performance and is in no way a devaluation of the person as a person.

The anger and hurt of the volunteer may have to be absorbed by the supervisor. It is to be hoped that in an organization devoted to human services, continuing pastoral care would be given to the offended worker, if possible, and if it seems that such care could be accepted.

Keep Service Records

Supervision and celebration are both made more effective by the maintenance of adequate records of volunteer service. These are in addition to the talent bank. The California Volunteer Network has suggested the following minimal records:[1]

Volunteer Program Records
1. Enrollment Records—
   Individual Volunteers
   a. All individual volunteers shall be registered with the agency/organization

[1]The California Volunteer Network, "Volunteer Program Planning: Direct Services Volunteer Program Standards," *Voluntary Action Leadership* (Fall, 1978), p. 28. Reprinted with permission. Copyright 1978 by the National Center for Voluntary Action.

served by means of a volunteer enrollment form which shall contain the
following personal information:
>   Name
>   Address
>   Phone
>   Date of enrollment
>   Birth date (if under 18)
>   Person to notify in emergency
>   Signature

b. If the volunteer may be called upon to
drive during the course of assignment,
the following information also must be
included:
>   Verification of valid driver's license
>   Expiration date
>   Insurance company of volunteer if
>   driving own car

c. Other information may be included on
the enrollment form when required to
meet agency/organization policies or
volunteer program requirements.

2. Enrollment Records—Volunteer Groups

a. Groups providing services to the agency or to clients of the agency will be
enrolled by means of a group enrollment form which shall contain the following minimal information:
>   Name of group
>   Name of group chairperson
>   Phone number of group chairperson
>   Service to be given
>   Date and time of service to be given
>   Names of members of group who
>   participate in providing service

b. Additional information may be included on the enrollment form when required by the agency/organization to
meet agency/organization or volunteer
program needs.

3. Volunteer Service Records and Reports

a. A running record of volunteer assignments shall be maintained. Such records shall contain at least the following
information:
>   Type of assignment
>   Work performed
>   Hours served
>   Performance evaluation
>   Person responsible for supervision

b. All injuries sustained by volunteers
while on assignment shall be reported
in writing to the agency/organization
executive.

c. All volunteer records are to be treated
as confidential personnel records.

d. Provisions shall be made to assure that
records are accessible to volunteers for
at least five years after termination,
and verification and quality of service
shall be provided at the volunteer's
request.

A sample record form is displayed at the end of
the chapter.

In Summary

The Body of Christ exists for ministry to the
world. As all bodies which remain healthy and
grow in strength, attention to maintenance and to
development is required. Maintenance and development through supervision is a way to build
up the Body of Christ. The talent, through the
gifts of the Spirit, is there. The role of the supervisor or enabler or professional minister is to
nurture the Body into fullness of being.

Sample Regular Individual Volunteer Record

Personnel Data

1. Mr.   Last Name   First   Middle Initial   Husband's Name   2. Birth Date
   Mrs.
   Miss

3. Address   Zip Code   4. Home Phone   Business Phone

5. Student Name of School   Campus Address   Zip Code

6. In Emergency Notify

Master Service Record

Cumulative Total Hours	Year 19 to 19	Total Hours	Cumulative Total Hours	Year 19 to 19	Total Hours	Cumulative Total Hours	Year 19 to 19	Total Hours
Month	Service	Hours	Month	Service	Hours	Month	Service	Hours

Bibliography

American Baptist National Ministries, *Ministry of the Laity Packet*, 1979. Available from Board of National Ministries, American Baptist Churches, Valley Forge, PA 19481.

American Baptist Women, *How-To Packet of Leadership Skills*. Available through Literature Service of Judson Book Stores, Valley Forge, PA 19481; 670 E. Butterfield Rd., Lombard, IL 60148; 816 S. Figueroa St., Los Angeles, CA 90017.

Arthur, Julietta K., *Retire to Action: A Guide to Voluntary Service*. Nashville: Abingdon Press, 1969.

Clingan, Donald F., *Aging Persons in the Community of Faith: A Guidebook for Churches and Synagogues on Ministry to, for, and with the Aging*. St. Louis: Christian Board of Publications, 1975.

Cohen, Lily, and Oppedisano-Reich, Marie, *Funding Sources in Aging: Public, Private, and Voluntary*. Garden City, N.Y.: Adelphi University Press, 1979.

Cull, John G., and Hardy, Richard E., eds., *Volunteerism: An Emerging Profession*. Springfield, Ill.: Charles C. Thomas, Publisher, 1974.

Enk, Mary J., and Hendricks, Marjorie, *Lighten Your Load with Volunteers*. Secaucus, N.J.: Lyle Stuart, Inc., 1976.

Fritz, Dan, *The Changing Retirement Scene: A Challenge for Decision Makers*. Los Angeles: University of Southern California Andrus Gerontology Center, 1978.

Heusser, D-B, *Helping Church Workers Succeed: The Enlistment and Support of Volunteers*. Valley Forge: Judson Press, 1980.

Jacobson, Ann, *Standards and Guidelines for the Field of Volunteerism*. Alexandria, Va.: Association of Volunteer Bureaus, 1978.

Johnson, Douglas W., *The Care and Feeding of Volunteers*. Nashville: Abingdon Press, 1978.

Lauffer, Armand, and Gorodezky, Sarah, *Volunteers*, Human Services Guides, vol. 5. Beverly Hills, Calif.: Sage Publications, Inc., 1977.

Manser, Gordon, and Cass, Rosemary H., *Voluntarism at the Crossroads*. New York: Family Service Association of America, 1976.

McClellan, Robert W., *Claiming a Frontier: Ministry and Older People*. Los Angeles: University of Southern California Andrus Gerontology Center, 1977.

National Center for Citizen Involvement, *Religion and Volunteering: A Notebook*. Boulder, Colo.: National Center for Citizen Involvement, 1978.

National Council of the YMCA, *Training Volunteer Leaders: A Handbook to Train Volunteers and Other Leaders of Program Groups,* 1974. Published by the Research and Development Division of YMCA—with Malcolm Knowles, Stanley Levin, and Eva Schindler-Rainman, consultants—this manual is available from the publisher at 291 Broadway, New York, NY 10007.

Naylor, Harriet H., *Volunteers Today: Finding, Training and Working with Them,* 1973. Available from Dryden Associates, Box 363, Dryden, NY 13053.

Office of Church Life and Leadership, United Church of Christ, *The Ministry of Volunteers: A Guidebook for Churches.* Seven thoroughly prepared training manuals guiding the church's volunteer ministry program, which can be ordered separately. They are *The Church and Its Volunteers, Volunteers and Volunteer Ministries, Developing a Mission Statement, Training Volunteers, Supporting Volunteers, Completing Volunteer Ministries,* and *Guiding the Church's Volunteer Ministry.* Available from Church Leadership Resources, P. O. Box 179, St. Louis, MO 63166.

Payne, Barbara P., ''The Older Volunteer: Social Role Continuity and Development,'' *The Gerontologist,* vol. 17, no. 4 (August, 1977), pp. 355-361.

Peckham, Charles W., and Arline B., *Thank You for Shaking My Hand: A Guidebook for Volunteers and Those Who Train or Direct Them in the Long-Term Care Facility.* Nashville: Parthenon Press, 1977.

Pell, Arthur R., *Recruiting, Training and Motivating Volunteer Workers.* New York: Pilot Books, 1977.

Pfeiffer, J. W., and Jones, J. E., *A Handbook of Structured Experiences for Human Relations Training,* vols. 1, 2, and 3. San Diego, Calif.: University Associates, 1973-1979.

Robertson, D. B., ed., *Voluntary Associations.* Richmond, Va.: John Knox Press, 1966.

Scheitlin, George E., and Gillstrom, Eleanor L., *Recruiting and Developing Volunteer Leaders.* Boulder, Colo.: National Center for Citizen Involvement, 1979.

Schindler, Arlene, and Chastain, Dale, *Volunteerism: Part of the Solution.* A discussion manual prepared for American Baptist Men and available through Literature Services of Judson Book Stores.

Schindler-Rainman, Eva, and Lippitt, Ronald, *The Volunteer Community: Creative Uses of Human Resources,* 2nd ed. Fairfax, Va.: NTL Learning Resources Corporation, 1971, 1975.

Smith, David H., *Voluntary Action Research.* Lexington, Mass.: Lexington Books, div. of D.C. Heath & Company, 1972.

Stenzel, Anne K., and Feeney, Helen M., *Volunteer Training and Development: A Manual.* New York: The Seabury Press, Inc., 1976.

University of Southern California Andrus Gerontology Center, *Releasing the Potential of Older Volunteers.* Los Angeles: University of Southern California Andrus Gerontology Center, 1976.

Wilson, Marlene, *The Effective Management of Volunteer Programs.* Boulder, Colo.: Volunteer Management Association, 1976.

Organizations Concerned with Volunteers

National Center for Citizen Involvement
P.O. Box 4179, Boulder, CO 80306 (303) 447-0492
or
1214 16th Street, NW, Washington, DC 20036 (202) 467-5560

Created in 1979 through a merger of the National Center for Voluntary Action and the National Center on Volunteerism, the National Center for Citizen Involvement publishes a quarterly journal, *Voluntary Action Leadership;* a bimonthly newsletter on advocacy, "Volunteering"; and a bimonthly newsletter on program activities, "Newsline." It also provides information services and leadership development. It is an agency of national voluntary organizations.

Association of Volunteer Bureaus
801 North Fairfax Street, Alexandria, VA 22314

More than three hundred cities have Voluntary Action Centers, usually supported by the United Way, which coordinate the recruitment and placement and training of volunteers. Many of them have an information and referral service. Often they administer the Retired Senior Volunteer Program (RSVP). These centers can provide consultation and training for local voluntary agencies.

These centers support the Association of Volunteer Bureaus which promotes the development and effective operation of local centers in line with national standards. A "Directory of Volunteer Bureaus and Voluntary Action Centers" is available as well as "Standards and Guidelines for the Field of Voluntarism." They also make available a film, "Let the Spirit Free," which can be rented for five dollars.

Guidelines for Proposal Writing

Funding Sources Service

(Used by permission of the Westside Ecumenical Ministry to the Elderly, 165 W. 84th St., New York, NY 10027.)

Most public agencies provide specific application forms and proposal guidelines which must be carefully followed in the preparation of an application document. Most private foundations do not, but some list a series of questions to be answered in the written proposal.

These guidelines have been prepared as *an aid* to the organization as it prepares a written presentation to submit to a private foundation.

A written proposal should demonstrate that the idea for your project is not only *important*, but that it meets a very *significant need*. In addition, the proposal should indicate why the applicant organization is the *most qualified* to make the project a success and that it has done a *thorough research* job of choosing the best solution to the existing problem. The most important component of a proposal is the *program description*, that part of the document which explains what the project entails. The proposal should also include an evaluation section—how the success of the project will be documented and measured. Finally, *future funding* for the project needs to be adequately identified and explained in the written presentation.

Remember, there is no one design or method of preparing a written proposal. However, this document in many instances will be the deciding factor in determining whether your organization will receive a grant. The following are the major components of a written proposal. You need to decide which sections *are relevant for you* to include in your written presentation.

MAJOR COMPONENTS OF A PROPOSAL

A. *Project Title* — Self-explanatory and brief.

B. *Summary Statement of the Proposal* — This statement should come near the beginning of the written presentation. It should contain information about the purposes of the project, how much it will cost, how long it will last, the state of readiness.

91

C. *Mission Statement*

This section should be stated in very specific terms. You should identify the needs, define the population and who will be served, and the geographic area in which the program will operate. It describes the importance of the problem and the investigative and verifying data that demonstrate the importance of what is proposed. Show the innovativeness and timeliness of the project and its solution; and finally [show] how the project is relevant elsewhere.

D. *Statement of Goals*

This section describes what the program seeks to achieve (long-range); who is to be served by the programs and the means to be utilized (staff, facilities).

E. *Statement of Objectives*

In this section the purpose of each activity is stated and the target date for its accomplishment. Objectives have a short-range timetable. They would be stated in measurable terms. If achievement of an objective is not measurable, it should be observable (e.g., one hundred adoptive evaluations per worker per year which result in fifty adoptive placements).

F. *Implementation, including Procedures*

In this section there should be a narrative description of how the project will work, including its management

and Organization

and organizational structure. This description should demonstrate your organization's ability to carry out the objectives you have stated.

G. *Evaluation*

This information should relate to each objective and its measurement. This section should contain the criteria to be used in each measurement, the data to be collected, and the method for collection. It provides the means to measure the results of the project and what has been accomplished.

H. *Dissemination*

In this section, you should state how the results of the project are going to be shared with other organizations. You might also include a description of the method and means of your reporting the funding source.

I. *Facilities*

Give a description of the physical facilities and special equipment that you feel is necessary to carry out the project.

J. *Personnel*

State how many employees, and in what categories (secretaries, consultants, professionals, etc.), will be required to carry out the project. If certain personnel will require special skills, these should be stated. (Job descriptions)

K. *Budget*

This section includes the total cost of the project

broken down by special categories (Personnel, Facilities, Materials, Administrative Costs, etc.). You should also include your organization's contribution in cash or in services.

Summary

Hints to keep in mind when soliciting foundations

Name and address of tax-exempt organization that will be the recipient if a grant is made.

Amount asked and specific purpose.

Significance—that is, what the grant is expected to accomplish.

The need or problem, including the background.

The proposed solution and method of approach to the problem (in the case of scientific research, the hypothesis).

Use to which the funding will be put, including plans to publish or publicize results.

Relationship of this proposal to the foundation's program as discernible in its recent published reports.

Endorsement of request by qualified individuals.

A detailed budget showing how the requested grant will be spent.

Length of time for which the foundation's aid will be needed. Include a schedule indicating most desirable time to start and terminate grant.

If staff is to be increased to carry out this project, what qualifications will be required and what evidence is there such staff is available?

Concise presentation of the essential facts. Usually a two- or three-page summary is adequate. A long memorandum and exhibits may accompany the summary if the applicant thinks these will strengthen his [or her] case. (A concise and forceful statement of these facts has more persuasive value than the format of the presentation.)

A copy of the ruling from the U.S. Treasury granting federal tax exemption.

If applicant organization has been active for a period of years, it would be well to provide a supplemental memorandum, indicating in brief the organization's accomplishments to date, the nature and extent of current and earlier support as well as the record of balances or deficits of past years.

A list of the organization's board of directors should be included with all requests.

If the organization has recently moved, make sure that the address and telephone number on the letterhead are current.

If a request has been submitted to a foundation and another funding source in the interim agrees to fund the same project, inform the first funding source.

In preparation for a meeting with a representative of a foundation, consult with that person as to who should be in attendance from the agency at the meeting.

Prepare a list of questions before you call a foundation representative regarding your proposal. Limit the number of calls you make to a funding source.